# UNDERSTANDING THE GREEN INDUSTRIAL REVOLUTION

*****

# An Interdisciplinary Look at the Hospitality industry

# Contents

**FOREWORD** ............................................................................................................. 6

**PREFACE** ................................................................................................................. 8

**CHAPTER 1: INTRODUCTION TO THE GREEN INDUSTRIAL REVOLUTION** ........ 13

    1.1 OVERVIEW OF THE GREEN INDUSTRIAL REVOLUTION AND ITS SIGNIFICANCE ............ 14

    1.2 EXPLORATION OF THE ENVIRONMENTAL AND ECONOMIC CHALLENGES THAT DRIVE THE NEED FOR GREENER TECHNOLOGIES ................................................................. 17

    1.3 THE UNITED STATES' GOAL OF REACHING NET NEUTRALITY BY 2050 AND THE CONSTRAINTS IT FACES ......................................................................................... 20

    1.4 CASE STUDIES SHOWCASING SUCCESSFUL GREEN INITIATIVES IN VARIOUS INDUSTRIES .. 32

    CONCLUSION ........................................................................................................ 37

**CHAPTER 2: UNDERSTANDING THE HOSPITALITY INDUSTRY** .......................... 38

    INTRODUCTION TO THE HOSPITALITY INDUSTRY AND ITS CURRENT ENVIRONMENTAL IMPACT 38

    2.1   A MULTI-DIMENSIONAL ANALYSIS FOR A SUSTAINABLE FUTURE ........................... 39

    2.2   IDENTIFYING OPPORTUNITIES FOR SUSTAINABILITY AND GREEN PRACTICES IN THE HOSPITALITY SECTOR ............................................................................................. 44

**CHAPTER 3: GREEN TECHNOLOGIES IN THE HOSPITALITY INDUSTRY** .......... 63

    INTRODUCTION TO VARIOUS GREEN TECHNOLOGIES AND THEIR APPLICATIONS ............ 63

    RENEWABLE ENERGY SYSTEMS ............................................................................ 64

    3.2   EXAMINING THE CURRENT TECHNOLOGY LANDSCAPE IN THE HOSPITALITY INDUSTRY 71

    3.3   ENERGY-EFFICIENT SOLUTIONS: RENEWABLE ENERGY SOURCES, ENERGY MANAGEMENT SYSTEMS, AND SMART GRIDS ................................................................................ 77

    3.4   WASTE REDUCTION AND RECYCLING TECHNOLOGIES ............................................ 79

    3.5   WATER CONSERVATION AND MANAGEMENT SOLUTIONS ....................................... 81

    3.6   ADVANTAGES AND CHALLENGES OF ADOPTING GREEN TECHNOLOGIES IN THE HOSPITALITY SECTOR ............................................................................................. 82

    CONCLUSION ........................................................................................................ 90

**CHAPTER 4: COMPARING GREEN TECHNOLOGIES TO GAS COUNTERPARTS** __ 91

    4.1   COMPARATIVE ANALYSIS OF TRADITIONAL GAS TECHNOLOGIES VERSUS GREENER ALTERNATIVES ....................................................................................................... 91

    4.2   COST BENEFIT ANALYSIS: EVALUATING IMMEDIATE COSTS AGAINST FUTURE GAINS AND ADVANTAGES .................................................................................................. 97

    4.3   ENVIRONMENTAL IMPACT ASSESSMENT: CARBON FOOTPRINT, POLLUTION, AND RESOURCE CONSUMPTION ..................................................................................... 102

CONCLUSION _____ 106

## CHAPTER 5: ENERGY EFFICIENCY IN HOSPITALITY OPERATIONS _____ 108

5.1 Energy-efficient lighting solutions: LED, motion sensors, and daylight harvesting _____ 109
5.2 Heating, ventilation, and air conditioning (HVAC) systems: energy-saving techniques and smart controls _____ 112
5.3 Efficient kitchen equipment and appliances _____ 113
5.4 Integrating Automation and Smart Technology for Energy Optimization in the Hospitality Industry _____ 117
5.5 Influence of ENERGY STAR© Product Certification & Benchmarking _____ 118
5.6 LEED Certification & Its Importance in the Hospitality Industry _____ 129
5.7 EcoChef Certification: Pioneering a Decarbonized Future in the Hospitality Industry _____ 135
5.8 The Impact of WELL Certification on the Hospitality Industry _____ 145
5.9 The Influence of ILFI on the Hospitality Industry _____ 149
5.10 The Role of BREEAM Certification in the Hospitality Industry _____ 152
5.11 Summary: The Convergence of Certification & Sustainability in the Hospitality Industry _____ 155

## CHAPTER 6: WASTE REDUCTION/DIVERSION AND RECYCLING STRATEGIES _____ 158

6.1 Waste management systems: recycling, composting, and waste-to-energy technologies _____ 159
6.2 Strategies for Reducing Food Waste in Hospitality Operations _____ 160
6.3 Waste Diversion Strategies: A Hands-On Approach for Chefs & Hospitality Professionals _____ 163
6.4 Sustainable procurement and packaging practices _____ 164
6.5 Involving Chefs, Staff, & Guests in Sustainable Waste Management _____ 166

## CHAPTER 7: WORKER HEALTH AND WELL-BEING IN THE HOSPITALITY INDUSTRY _____ 169

7.1 The Symbiotic Relationship Between Worker Well-Being & Sustainable Hospitality _____ 169
7.2 Understanding the unique challenges and risks faced by hospitality workers _____ 172
7.3 Navigating Occupational Hazards & Health Issues in the Hospitality Industry Amidst the Green Industrial Revolution _____ 174
7.4 Ergonomic Considerations in Sustainable Hospitality Workplaces _____ 179
Conclusion _____ 180

## CHAPTER 8: OVERCOMING CHALLENGES IN GREEN TECHNOLOGY ADOPTION ............ 181

8.1 BARRIERS AND CHALLENGES TO IMPLEMENTING GREEN TECHNOLOGIES IN THE HOSPITALITY INDUSTRY ............ 182
8.2 STRATEGIES FOR OVERCOMING BARRIERS TO GREEN TECHNOLOGY ADOPTION ___ 184
8.3 COLLABORATIONS & PARTNERSHIPS FOR ADVANCING SUSTAINABLE INNOVATION IN THE HOSPITALITY SECTOR ............ 188
CONCLUSION ............ 189

## CHAPTER 9: ECONOMIC BENEFITS OF GREEN TECHNOLOGIES ............ 191

9.1 EXPLORING THE ECONOMIC ADVANTAGES OF ADOPTING GREEN TECHNOLOGIES IN THE HOSPITALITY INDUSTRY ............ 192
9.2 RETURN ON INVESTMENT (ROI) ANALYSIS AND COST SAVINGS FROM ENERGY AND RESOURCE EFFICIENCY ............ 194
9.3 BRAND ENHANCEMENT AND MARKET POSITIONING THROUGH SUSTAINABLE PRACTICES 195
CONCLUSION ............ 197

## CHAPTER 10: POLICY AND REGULATIONS DRIVING GREEN REVOLUTION ___ 199

10.1 OVERVIEW OF U.S. NATIONAL POLICIES PROMOTING GREEN TECHNOLOGIES AND SUSTAINABILITY ............ 199
10.2 OVERVIEW OF INTERNATIONAL POLICIES PROMOTING GREEN TECHNOLOGIES AND SUSTAINABILITY ............ 202
10.3 UNDERSTANDING REGULATORY FRAMEWORKS AND INCENTIVES: NAVIGATING THE PATH TO GREEN HOSPITALITY ............ 206
10.4 CASE STUDIES ON SUCCESSFUL POLICY IMPLEMENTATIONS AND THEIR TRANSFORMATIVE IMPACTS ............ 208
CONCLUSION ............ 210

## CHAPTER 11: CASE STUDIES: SUCCESSFUL GREEN TRANSFORMATIONS IN HOSPITALITY ............ 212

11.1 EXAMINING REAL-WORLD EXAMPLES OF HOSPITALITY'S EMBRACING OF GREEN TECHNOLOGIES ............ 213
11.2 LESSONS LEARNED & BEST PRACTICES FROM SUSTAINABLE HOTELS, RESORTS, & RESTAURANTS ............ 217
11.3 ADVANCING SUSTAINABLE HOSPITALITY: FROM INNOVATION TO IMPLEMENTATION 220
CONCLUSION ............ 223

## CHAPTER 12: FUTURE TRENDS AND OPPORTUNITIES IN THE GREEN INDUSTRIAL REVOLUTION ............ 225

12.1 Emerging Trends and Technologies in the Green Industrial Revolution 226
12.2 Potential Challenges and Opportunities in the Future of the Hospitality Industry 229
12.3 Building a Holistic Sustainable Model: Interdisciplinary Approaches & Stakeholder Involvement _____ 232

**APPENDIX: ADDITIONAL RESOURCES & TERMINOLOGY_____ 236**

# FOREWORD

From the perilous streets of New Jersey to the high-energy kitchens of a 5-star, 5-diamond resort, my journey has been anything but conventional. As a first-generation American, I grew up amid violence and loss. But, through well-timed decisions by my incredible mother, I was guided towards the culinary arts—a decision that would fundamentally alter the trajectory of my life. My early days were spent copying the entire textbook from the Culinary Institute of America in a desperate attempt to self-educate before embarking on formal education. It was during this educational journey that I met Kristina, the love of my life. My time, working for a world-renowned Certified Master Chef, as an apprentice at the Greenbrier was instrumental, not just in honing my skills but also in meeting Chef Gerard T. Kenny II, a dear friend and collaborator who has been vital in my journey.

While managing America's first all-electric campus kitchen at the world's first fully self-sustained university campus at Chatham University's Eden Hall Campus, I unearthed a second love: sustainability and kitchen electrification. A phone call from Katie Ross at Microsoft was a pivotal moment that opened new vistas in my career. It introduced me to a fascinating intersection of sustainability and the hospitality industry. This led to the creation of Forward Dining Solutions, which eventually positioned me as the nation's leading expert in commercial kitchen electrification and decarbonization. This has been more than a pivot; it's become my life's work, a mission to bring a holistic and humane change to an industry known for its demands on mental and physical health.

Forward Dining Solutions aims to change not just how kitchens function but how the industry thinks. It's a revolution in the making, aiming to replace outdated, harmful practices with innovative, sustainable solutions. Our vision is to create an industry that is as compassionate as it is efficient, without losing sight of the environmental implications. The technology is here, the will is growing, and the need is undeniable. This revolution isn't just about today; it's about setting a precedent for future generations.

I would be remiss if I did not express my heartfelt gratitude towards two crucial people in my life—my fiancée, Kristina Mason, and my friend and business partner, Gerard T. Kenny II. Kristina, your love and support have been my anchor, making this challenging journey not just possible but worthwhile. Gerard, your friendship and partnership have been invaluable in realizing the vision and mission of Forward Dining Solutions.

This book is more than a mere guide; it's a call to action. In these pages, I hope to inspire you to join us in this essential transformation of the hospitality industry. Let's build a sustainable future together, for the hospitality veterans of today and the generations of tomorrow.

Chef Christopher A. Galarza

Founder& CEO

Forward Dining Solutions

# PREFACE

Welcome to "Understanding the Green Industrial Revolution: An Interdisciplinary Look at the Hospitality Industry," the essential companion to your course on the transformative potential of the green industrial revolution. This book offers a nuanced exploration of how the emerging era of sustainable technologies is revolutionizing various industries, focusing particularly on its impact within the hospitality sector.

**A Time of Transition**

We find ourselves in a critical juncture, a transition period that holds the power to redefine the human relationship with our planet. This isn't just an environmental issue but a confluence of technological innovation, social responsibility, and economic pragmatism. The "green industrial revolution" is far more than a mere catchphrase—it represents a comprehensive and urgent shift in how industries operate, how governments regulate, and how communities participate in shaping their own future. It's an awakening to the reality that the old paradigms of industrialization, built on fossil fuel consumption and unrestrained exploitation of natural resources, are no longer sustainable.

The stakes are high, especially considering the irreversible impacts of climate change, diminishing natural resources, and increasing social inequities. In this backdrop, the green industrial revolution offers a framework for change, a pathway to reorient industrial ecosystems around principles of sustainability, social equity, and economic viability. No sector is untouched by this monumental shift, and the hospitality industry, given its global reach and consumer-focused nature, stands at a fascinating crossroads. Will it cling to the status quo, or will it embrace change and set new standards for responsible, sustainable operation? This question is not just theoretical but one that industry leaders are grappling with right now.

As you navigate this textbook and your course, it's crucial to approach the subject matter with an awareness of this broader transition. The hospitality industry is not an isolated bubble but an integral part of global systems—economic, environmental, and social. Its transformation, or lack thereof, has implications that extend beyond hotel lobbies and vacation spots. The choices made within this sector can influence policy decisions, affect local and global ecosystems, and contribute to the societal mindset about what is acceptable or even possible in our collective approach to sustainability. We are all actors in this unfolding drama, and the time for action is now.

**Navigating Complexities**

The journey toward understanding the role of the green industrial revolution in reshaping the hospitality industry is fraught with complexities. These intricacies stem from multiple sources: the rapid pace of technological innovations, a maze of governmental regulations and incentives, shifting consumer preferences, and the intricacies of implementing change in established operational structures. It's not just about replacing traditional gas-operated systems with renewable energy sources; it's about an entire rethinking of how a business, an industry, and even a society should function. As we delve into these topics, it becomes apparent that a siloed approach, where each issue is considered in isolation, would be insufficient to capture the full picture.

The hospitality industry itself is a multifaceted entity, engaging with various stakeholders that include not just hotel owners and guests but also local communities, suppliers, regulatory bodies, and even the natural environment around a property. Each decision to adopt a new green technology or to implement a sustainable practice reverberates through this interconnected web of relationships. For instance, a move to source local organic produce for a hotel's restaurant doesn't just reduce carbon emissions related to transportation; it also impacts local agriculture, potentially invigorating community-based economies. Likewise, the implementation of energy-efficient systems in hotel operations might meet environmental objectives but can also require comprehensive staff training, thus implicating human resource dynamics.

But complexities should not be seen as impediments; rather, they offer a rich tapestry of opportunities for learning, innovation, and leadership. Each challenge presents a chance to dig deeper, to ask more thoughtful questions, and to develop more effective, holistic solutions. Our exploration will require us to engage critically with these complexities, not to simplify them, but to better understand the rich network of factors that will define the future of the hospitality industry—and by extension, contribute to the shaping of a more sustainable and equitable global society. As students, professionals, or simply as conscientious individuals, mastering the art of navigating these complexities is not just an academic exercise but a crucial skillset for meaningful participation in the world of tomorrow.

## What Will You Learn?

This textbook aims to be more than a repository of facts and case studies; it aspires to be a catalyst for change. As you navigate through the chapters, you'll engage with a multifaceted understanding of the green industrial revolution and its far-reaching implications on the hospitality industry. We'll start by unpacking the core concepts behind this transformative movement, from sustainability metrics to the technologies driving renewable energy and waste management. By anchoring these global themes in the specific context of the hospitality industry, we offer a unique lens through which to view these revolutionary shifts. You'll learn not just what these changes are, but how they work, why they matter, and who is leading the way in implementing them.

Beyond a theoretical framework, this course empowers you to become a proactive contributor to this ongoing revolution. Through real-world case studies, you'll see firsthand the challenges and triumphs of implementing green technologies in the hospitality sector. You'll dissect the economic, social, and environmental impacts of these initiatives, arming you with the knowledge and perspective to make informed decisions in your future roles—be it as hospitality professionals, policymakers, or conscious consumers. Moreover, the course is designed to hone your critical thinking and problem-solving skills, encouraging you to look beyond surface-level data to understand the underlying complexities and ethical considerations.

So, what will you learn? You'll learn to be an agent of change in a world desperate for solutions. You'll learn that the green industrial revolution is not just a trend but a necessary shift towards a sustainable future—and you can be a part of it. By the end of this book, you won't just understand the changing landscape of the hospitality industry; you'll be inspired to lead it. Let this textbook be your guide, your reference, and your inspiration as you step into a world of untold possibilities, a world that you have the power to shape for the better. Welcome to a journey of discovery, transformation, and impact. Welcome to your future.

# Chapter 1

# Introduction to the Green Industrial Revolution

This inaugural chapter serves as an entry point into the rapidly evolving landscape of sustainability in the hospitality industry. Against the backdrop of the Green Industrial Revolution—a transformative movement aimed at melding economic growth with ecological responsibility—this chapter lays the groundwork for understanding how the hospitality sector is uniquely positioned to contribute to a more sustainable future. As consumers increasingly align their values with eco-conscious travel and responsible consumption, hospitality providers face both challenges and opportunities. This chapter will introduce the core concepts, frameworks, and key trends that are driving sustainable practices in the industry, setting the stage for deeper explorations in subsequent chapters.

# 1.1 Overview of the green industrial revolution and its significance

The Green Industrial Revolution is not just a buzzword; it's a pressing necessity. With the looming challenges of climate change, the call for a greener shift in industrial practices is reaching a crescendo. The urgency is echoed not only by climate scientists but also by architects designing energy-efficient buildings, engineers crafting sustainable technologies, and chefs advocating for low-impact culinary practices. In this vein, let's explore the various dimensions that make the Green Industrial Revolution a subject of paramount importance.

## Climate Urgency

One of the most compelling motivators behind the Green Industrial Revolution is the stark reality of climate change. From record-breaking temperatures to devastating storms, the evidence for a rapidly changing climate is becoming difficult to ignore. For the hospitality sector, which is the specific focus of this book, climate change poses unique challenges—be it the scarcity of water affecting resort destinations or extreme weather affecting seasonal businesses.

## Environmental Sustainability

The Green Industrial Revolution doesn't just stop at addressing climate change. It is intrinsically linked with the broader goal of environmental sustainability. Whether it's architects employing bio-friendly materials or chefs using sustainably sourced ingredients, every profession can contribute to broader environmental goals. These include reducing pollution, conserving biodiversity, and adopting better land and water management practices. For the hospitality industry, this could manifest in sustainable waste management and electrified energy-efficient kitchens, among other practices.

## Economic Resilience

Politicians and economists are increasingly realizing the economic viability and necessity of going green. Sustainable practices are not just ethically responsible choices but also financially sound investments. Many governments, including the United States, have made it a goal to achieve carbon neutrality by 2050. However, the path is rife with challenges, from existing fossil fuel infrastructure to political roadblocks. The hospitality industry, with its significant carbon footprint, especially in its kitchens, faces its own set of unique challenges and opportunities in this transition.

## Health Benefits

The pivot toward greener technologies is accompanied by a cascading effect of health benefits that are often under-discussed but profoundly impactful. For example, the reduction in fossil fuel emissions leads to improved air quality, which in turn minimizes the risks of respiratory ailments such as asthma, bronchitis, and even certain types of cancer. Transitioning away from chemical-intensive agricultural and cleaning products reduces exposure to harmful substances, which can mitigate skin conditions, allergic reactions, and long-term risks of hormonal imbalances. In the hospitality sector, this can translate to cleaner air in hotels and resorts, as well as the use of organic and non-toxic cleaning agents and cooking supplies in kitchens, creating a healthier environment for both employees and guests.

Further extending the health benefits are the psychological well-being aspects that come with a greener environment. Numerous studies have shown that green spaces and natural settings can reduce stress, anxiety, and even symptoms of depression. In this context, imagine the positive mental health impact of a sustainably managed resort surrounded by preserved natural beauty. Such an environment not only contributes to guest satisfaction but also enhances the well-being of the people working there. By weaving sustainability into its core operations, the hospitality industry can serve as a microcosm for how the Green Industrial Revolution can uplift overall health—physically and mentally—for society at large.

## Technological Innovation and International Collaboration

The Green Industrial Revolution isn't just about incremental changes; it often involves leaps in innovation that fundamentally reshape industries. Engineers, scientists, and product developers are pushing the envelope in creating solutions that are not only environmentally friendly but also highly efficient. In the world of hospitality, nowhere is this more evident than in kitchen technologies, which are a significant part of the industry's carbon footprint. Induction cooking, for instance, is drastically more energy-efficient compared to traditional gas stoves. It allows for faster and more precise cooking, leading to less energy waste. Similarly, combination ovens, which integrate convection and steam cooking, offer flexibility and efficiency, allowing chefs to cook multiple types of dishes at once without compromising on quality or energy use.

These technological advances are not isolated; they are part of a global tapestry of innovation spurred by the Green Industrial Revolution. As these technologies become mainstream, they pave the way for international collaboration, where best practices and advancements are shared across borders. For instance, a sustainable kitchen innovation developed in a European culinary institute could easily find its way to a high-end resort in Asia, amplifying the positive environmental impact worldwide. This synergy between technological innovation and international cooperation is one of the defining features of the Green Industrial Revolution, creating a loop of continuous improvement that benefits not just individual industries like hospitality but society at large.

## 1.2 Exploration of the Environmental and Economic challenges that drive the need for greener technologies

### Environmental Challenges

The Green Industrial Revolution is an inspiring leap forward for society, serving both as an ecological safeguard and an economic catalyst. Over the last several decades, a variety of environmental challenges have underscored the urgent need for this transformative shift, accelerating global efforts towards sustainable practices.

- *Climate Change and Global Warming:* These twin challenges are at the forefront of the environmental issues driving the transition to greener technologies. The hospitality sector, with its global reach, is uniquely affected by these changes, which impact everything from food supply chain sustainability for kitchens to energy efficiency needs.
- *Resource Depletion:* Traditional sectors, including hospitality, have often been heavy users of non-renewable resources. For example, commercial kitchens have been

reliant on natural gas for cooking, contributing both to greenhouse gas emissions and resource depletion. Innovations like induction cooking offer a more sustainable path.

- *Air and Water Pollution*: The adverse health effects of pollution, particularly from industries that make heavy use of fossil fuels and chemicals, have been well-documented. This issue is of special concern to the hospitality industry, where high-energy kitchens and waste outputs can be significant contributors.
- *Waste Management:* Poor waste management strategies can lead to the degradation of natural habitats and contribute to global climate change. Within the hospitality industry, this calls for more sustainable waste management practices, such as composting food waste from kitchens and utilizing recyclable materials.

## Economic Factors

While environmental imperatives serve as the moral compass guiding us toward greener technologies, economic factors are the engine that powers this transformation. Often viewed as two separate realms, the economy and ecology are increasingly interconnected, each influencing the other in complex ways. Businesses, particularly in the hospitality sector, are recognizing that sustainability is not just an ethical choice but also a financially sound investment for long-term growth and risk mitigation. In the following subsections, we explore various economic drivers that are making the adoption of green technologies an increasingly compelling option for industries worldwide.

- *Cost Efficiency:* While the initial costs of transitioning to green technologies were seen as prohibitive, experience shows that the long-term savings can be substantial. Energy-efficient kitchen technologies like combination ovens and induction stoves can significantly reduce operational costs.
- *Government Regulations and Incentives:* Recognizing the urgent need for a sustainable transition, governments globally are introducing supportive policies, including regulations to curb emissions and waste, as well as financial incentives like grants, subsidies, and tax benefits.
- *Investor and Stakeholder Pressure:* As the business landscape evolves, investors and stakeholders are increasingly emphasizing sustainability when evaluating investment opportunities. For the hospitality industry, this means that green initiatives are not just ethical choices but also strong business strategies.
- *Consumer Demand:* A growing consumer focus on sustainability is also guiding the industry. For hospitality businesses, this translates into a burgeoning market for eco-friendly establishments, and kitchens that adopt green practices are often at the forefront of this demand.
- *Long-Term Viability and Risk Mitigation:* Embracing sustainable practices is increasingly seen as essential for long-term business success. Such measures not only decrease dependency on finite resources but also better prepare companies for market fluctuations and future regulatory changes.

In summary, the Green Industrial Revolution represents an essential and hopeful response to various pressing environmental and economic challenges. By embracing this transformation, industries like hospitality can contribute to building a more sustainable and prosperous future.

## 1.3 The United States' goal of reaching net neutrality by 2050 and the constraints it faces

In an era where urgency meets opportunity, the United States has taken a decisive step to lead by example, setting a landmark objective of achieving net carbon neutrality by 2050. Underpinned by Executive Order 14057, or "The Federal Sustainability Plan," this visionary roadmap isn't just a bureaucratic formality; it serves as a linchpin for transformative change. The plan integrates a spectrum of strategies and initiatives, meticulously designed to complement each other, as we collectively pivot toward a more sustainable, innovative, and inclusive future. This bold ambition does more than set new standards for environmental responsibility; it serves as a critical pillar in shaping a broader socio-economic transformation—a Green Industrial Revolution, if you will. This endeavor deeply aligns with the core tenets of this course, emphasizing the importance of integrating sustainability, technological innovation, and social inclusivity into our daily practices and long-term strategies.

By dissecting the multi-pronged approach laid out in the federal plan, this section aims to explore how these governmental commitments can become the springboard for wide-ranging advancements. These span from clean energy to green finance, and from resilient infrastructure to public awareness, painting a comprehensive picture of the future we aim to build. Through a lens of holistic understanding, we will delve into the intricate ways these strategies can permeate the hospitality industry and serve as a blueprint for collective action against climate change.

# Multi-Dimensional Strategies to Foster a Green Industrial Revolution

**1.** *Renewable Energy Investments*

As the quest for a sustainable future gains momentum, renewable energy investments emerge as a cornerstone in fostering a Green Industrial Revolution. The U.S. government, through its comprehensive Federal Sustainability Plan, acknowledges the irreplaceable role of clean energy sources such as solar, wind, hydro, and geothermal. These aren't merely alternatives; they're imperatives for reducing greenhouse gas emissions and mitigating the impacts of climate change. In line with the course's focus on technological innovation, it's noteworthy that advancements in renewable technologies have made them increasingly efficient and cost-effective. For instance, solar photovoltaic (PV) cells have seen exponential improvements in efficiency, while the costs have substantially declined.

The U.S. government's involvement transcends simple encouragement, acting as a catalyst by setting ambitious renewable energy targets that can serve as a beacon for private businesses. For example, tax incentives, subsidies, and even public-private partnerships can be harnessed to accelerate the development and deployment of these technologies. Within the hospitality industry, this could manifest as hotels integrating solar panels, using wind energy for operations, or even tapping into geothermal heating for pools and spas. Such initiatives not only lower the carbon footprint but also resonate with increasingly eco-conscious consumers, thereby fulfilling market demands for sustainability. By enhancing renewable energy infrastructure, the United States can set a course towards energy independence and a more sustainable future, effectively bridging the gap between ecological responsibility and economic viability.

## 2. *Carbon Pricing and Market Mechanisms*

Carbon pricing represents a market-based strategy that is critical in transitioning towards a Green Industrial Revolution. By introducing financial implications for emitting carbon, the government can create a compelling economic argument for industries to transition to greener technologies and practices. The course places a strong emphasis on economic drivers, and carbon pricing perfectly illustrates how economic mechanisms can encourage sustainable actions. Various models like carbon taxes and cap-and-trade systems can be implemented. In a cap-and-trade system, companies buy and sell emission allowances, thereby creating a financial incentive to reduce emissions below the cap. The revenue generated from these mechanisms can then be funneled back into the economy to fund other green initiatives, thereby creating a virtuous cycle of investment and improvement.

In the context of the hospitality industry, this could mean increased costs for those still relying on fossil fuels for their operations, effectively making it economically prudent to switch to renewable energy sources. Carbon pricing could also influence decisions around food sourcing, waste management, and overall operational efficiency. Hotels, for example, might find it more cost-effective to source local organic produce, which has a lower carbon footprint compared to imported goods. Additionally, these policies can inspire innovation, as companies strive to develop new technologies or practices that fall below the emission cap, thereby saving money and reducing their carbon footprint. As carbon pricing models become more widespread, they will play an increasingly crucial role in shaping a more sustainable future, fulfilling both environmental and economic objectives. This will encourage businesses, notably in hospitality, to adopt environmentally friendly technologies and sustainable practices, considering both ethical and economic implications.

**3.** *Green Finance and Sustainable Investments*

Green finance and sustainable investments have evolved into critical enablers of the Green Industrial Revolution, functioning as the economic engines that fund sustainable projects across sectors. Financial institutions are uniquely positioned to catalyze this change by providing much-needed capital to initiatives that prioritize environmental responsibility. In the course, we discuss the intricate relationship between economic imperatives and sustainable practices, and green finance embodies this nexus. Various financial instruments such as green bonds, sustainable loans, and impact investment funds are now available to direct significant capital flows towards eco-friendly projects.

For example, in the hospitality industry, green financing options can be pivotal in making the transition to renewable energy sources or implementing waste reduction strategies. Tax incentives, subsidies, or low-interest loans for installing solar panels, energy-efficient HVAC systems, or waste-to-energy technologies can significantly lower the initial financial hurdles. This form of financial backing is especially pertinent for larger corporations that have the clout to bring about substantial change. By incorporating environmental, social, and governance (ESG) criteria into investment and lending decisions, financial institutions can not only influence corporate behavior but also meet the growing demand from investors for more responsible and sustainable investment options. As these green finance mechanisms mature and proliferate, they are set to become a central pillar in the global push towards sustainability, effectively bridging the gap between economic viability and environmental stewardship.

## 4. *Circular Economy and Extended Producer Responsibility*

Embracing a circular economy model marks a profound shift from the traditional linear economic model of "take, make, dispose" to a more regenerative approach of "reduce, reuse, recycle." This transformation is not just an environmentally responsible choice; it's a vital business strategy, especially relevant to the hospitality industry. The old paradigm of using resources in a single direction, without considering their life after use, has proven unsustainable both environmentally and financially. In contrast, the circular model designs products and systems for longevity and multiple cycles of use, thereby significantly reducing waste and the demand for new raw materials.

Within the hospitality sector, adopting a circular economy can manifest in various strategies, ranging from mindful supply chain management to operational efficiencies. Hotels can enact extended producer responsibility by working with suppliers who take back packaging for reuse or recycling. Furnishings and appliances can be selected based on their durability and potential for repair, thereby extending their lifecycles. Food waste can be minimized through smart inventory management, and organic waste can be repurposed for composting or bioenergy. Furthermore, water recycling technologies can be integrated into the property's infrastructure, contributing to resource conservation.

The concept of extended producer responsibility amplifies the impact of a circular economy model. By partnering with producers who take responsibility for the full life cycle of their products, hotels can minimize their waste management burden and disposal costs. This is increasingly important to an eco-conscious consumer base that values sustainable practices. Through the integration of these principles, the hospitality industry not only mitigates its environmental impact but can also realize cost savings and meet the growing demand for sustainability from both consumers and stakeholders.

## 5. Electrification and Sustainable Transportation in the Hospitality Industry

Electrification and sustainable transportation options represent significant avenues for reducing carbon emissions, particularly within the hospitality sector. Hotels, resorts, and other establishments can greatly contribute to this objective by incorporating electric vehicles (EVs) into their fleet operations. Whether these are shuttle services to and from the airport/local destinations, or transporting off-site catering, using electric or hybrid vehicles will not only cut down on greenhouse gas emissions but also resonate with environmentally conscious guests.

Moreover, hotels and resorts can further this initiative by installing EV charging stations on their premises, encouraging both guests and employees to opt for cleaner transportation methods. This is not just an environmental advantage; it's an added service that can attract eco-minded guests and help earn a reputation for sustainable practices. By promoting walking, cycling, and the use of public transportation, businesses can extend their commitment to sustainable transport. Some upscale hotels even offer electric bikes or scooters to their guests, providing a fun, eco-friendly way to explore local attractions.

In the broader context, the adoption of sustainable transportation options can be considered part of a destination's attractiveness. Tourists are increasingly favoring destinations that make it easy to maintain a low carbon footprint. Hotels can partner with local authorities and businesses to develop integrated, sustainable transport solutions that will benefit not only the guests but also the community at large. By taking these steps, the hospitality industry can effectively reduce its transportation-related environmental impacts, enrich guest experiences, and contribute substantively to the Green Industrial Revolution.

**Electrification vs. Fossil Fuels:** Electrification, as opposed to traditional fossil fuels, offers a cleaner alternative for transportation by significantly reducing greenhouse gas emissions. Electric vehicles produce zero tailpipe emissions, thereby minimizing air pollution and combating climate change by utilizing cleaner energy sources.

By utilizing electricity as a power source, electric vehicles avoid the direct emissions associated with burning fossil fuels in internal combustion engines. Electricity generation can be sourced from renewable energy, such as solar or wind power, further reducing the carbon footprint of electric vehicles compared to vehicles running on gasoline or diesel.

The transition to electric transportation within the hospitality sector aligns with broader sustainability goals, offering a tangible way to mitigate environmental impacts associated with conventional fuel-powered vehicles. This shift not only reduces emissions but also contributes to creating a more sustainable and cleaner transportation ecosystem.

## 6. Reforestation and Conservation Efforts

Reforestation and conservation efforts have broad implications for the hospitality industry, extending beyond just hotels and resorts to include restaurants, event venues, and even travel agencies. One significant way the industry can contribute is by integrating these environmental priorities into their business models. For instance, restaurants could pledge to plant a tree for every certain number of meals sold, or travel agencies might include a small carbon offset fee that goes directly to reforestation projects. This not only aids in reducing the overall carbon footprint but also elevates the brand's image among eco-conscious consumers.

Venues for events and conferences can adopt conservation methods, such as the use of energy-efficient materials and waste reduction policies, and tie this into broader efforts like local reforestation projects. They can also use their platforms to educate attendees about the importance of conservation and sustainable living, thereby amplifying the impact. Collaboration is key; by partnering with environmental organizations, local communities, and even government bodies, businesses in the hospitality sector can participate in and sponsor reforestation efforts or habitat restoration projects. This can range from organizing community tree-planting events to restoring local parks and waterways. In doing so, the industry doesn't just minimize its own environmental impact but also enriches the communities they operate in, making them more attractive to potential visitors.

## 7. Technology Transfer and Capacity Building

The concept of technology transfer and capacity building holds immense promise for the hospitality sector, encompassing not just hotels and resorts but also restaurants, travel agencies, and entertainment venues. Adopting cleaner, more efficient technologies can result in substantial energy and cost savings across the board. For example, restaurants could implement energy-efficient kitchen equipment, sourced from countries with advanced green technologies, to reduce energy consumption and emissions. Similarly, travel agencies could integrate software that calculates the carbon footprint of various travel options, allowing consumers to make more informed, eco-friendly choices.

Capacity building is equally important. By investing in the training and development of employees on best sustainability practices and the use of green technologies, the hospitality industry can significantly amplify its positive environmental impact. This training can be done in-house or through partnerships with NGOs (non-governmental organizations) and educational institutions specialized in sustainability and technology. Moreover, industry-wide webinars, workshops, and conferences can serve as platforms to share knowledge about the latest in green technologies and sustainable practices. By equipping themselves with the right tools and knowledge, businesses in the hospitality industry not only contribute to environmental conservation but also position themselves as leaders in sustainable operation, thereby attracting a more conscientious clientele.

## 8. *Education and Awareness*

Education and awareness-raising are fundamental components in driving sustainable practices across the hospitality sector, which includes restaurants, travel services, event planning, and entertainment spaces, in addition to hotels and resorts. These businesses are uniquely positioned to educate a broad audience, including guests, suppliers, and employees, about the importance of sustainability. For instance, restaurants could incorporate digital menus that detail the carbon footprint of each meal, or offer sustainable, locally sourced alternatives. Travel agencies could provide educational material highlighting the environmental impact of different travel options, thereby nudging consumers towards more responsible choices like eco-friendly destinations or travel methods.

An educated staff is equally critical to this endeavor. Employee training programs that teach the importance of sustainability, the proper use of energy-efficient technologies, and waste management can make a significant impact. Awareness can also be elevated through promotional materials or in-app features that explain the company's sustainability initiatives and the tangible benefits they provide. By making sustainability an integral part of the customer experience, businesses in the hospitality sector can both meet the growing demand for environmentally conscious options and contribute meaningfully to global sustainability efforts.

9. *Green Innovation and Research*

Green innovation and research are cornerstones for advancing sustainable practices within the broader hospitality industry, including event planning, travel services, and entertainment venues, as well as the more traditional areas like hotels and restaurants. With the rapid technological advancements in sustainability, there's an opportunity for the industry to become pioneers in implementing new green technologies. For instance, event planners could use innovative, biodegradable materials for decoration and waste management, or invest in advanced audio-visual equipment that consumes less energy. Restaurants could embrace technologies such as induction cooking that can increase throughput while decreasing operational expenses and waste, or employ AI-powered solutions to better manage supply chain logistics for minimal carbon footprint.

Moreover, the hospitality industry can collaborate with research institutions and startups to develop technologies tailored to their unique sustainability challenges. Public-private partnerships can also prove instrumental in accelerating research and development in areas like energy-efficient kitchen appliances or eco-friendly cleaning solutions. Investing in green innovation not only reduces operational costs in the long run but also aligns the industry with consumer demands for more responsible and sustainable options. By actively participating in, or even leading, research efforts, the hospitality industry can contribute to the larger ecosystem of sustainability, gaining a competitive advantage and future-proofing their businesses.

## 10. *Resilient Infrastructure Planning*

Resilient infrastructure planning is a pivotal element in ensuring the long-term sustainability and operational effectiveness of the hospitality industry, including sectors like event spaces, restaurants, entertainment venues, and, of course, hotels and resorts. In the face of intensifying impacts of climate change such as rising sea levels, extreme weather events, and natural disasters, constructing or retrofitting venues with resilient materials and systems becomes crucial. For instance, event spaces could be designed with flood-resistant materials and features, while restaurants could invest in energy-efficient HVAC systems that can also serve as safe zones during extreme weather conditions.

The concept of resilient infrastructure also extends to supply chain and logistical planning, which are critical to the uninterrupted functioning of the hospitality industry. For example, food and beverage suppliers for restaurants and event spaces could be sourced locally to reduce transportation emissions and risks, and thereby, make the supply chain more resilient to potential disruptions caused by environmental factors. By incorporating resilience into infrastructure planning, the hospitality industry can not only minimize risks but also ensure its own long-term sustainability and financial viability, all while contributing to broader environmental goals.

## Challenges and Constraints in the Hospitality Industry

While the ambition to foster a Green Industrial Revolution within the hospitality sector is commendable, it is fraught with challenges that extend beyond hotels and resorts to include restaurants, event spaces, and entertainment venues. One of the most pressing challenges is the significant upfront financial investment required to make existing infrastructure more sustainable. Whether it's adopting energy-efficient systems or waste management solutions, initial costs can be prohibitive, especially for smaller establishments. Additionally, shifting to locally sourced or organic food in restaurants, or sustainable materials in event spaces, may increase operational costs, making it difficult to compete with less sustainable counterparts without passing the cost on to the consumer.

Another constraint is the complex nature of the supply chain in the hospitality industry. Many venues rely on a global network for their supplies, whether it's food, decor, or technology. While local sourcing is more sustainable, it may not always be feasible or may limit the range of offerings, affecting customer experience and satisfaction. Moreover, regulatory frameworks around sustainability are not uniform across jurisdictions, making it a challenge for establishments that operate in multiple locations to adhere to a consistent set of sustainable practices. Despite these challenges, the growing consumer demand for sustainability and the long-term cost savings that green practices can offer make it an imperative that the industry must strive to meet.

In the overarching quest to usher in a Green Industrial Revolution, the U.S. government has laid out a multi-faceted roadmap to reach carbon neutrality by 2050. These strategies range from renewable energy investments and market-based mechanisms like carbon pricing, to fostering green finance and sustainable transportation. Particularly in the hospitality industry, these approaches carry a unique set of implications and opportunities. However, achieving these ambitious goals is not without challenges, including financial constraints and supply chain complexities. Despite these hurdles, the movement towards sustainability is not just a government objective but a collective responsibility, one that is increasingly recognized and demanded by consumers.

## 1.4 Case studies showcasing successful green initiatives in various industries

### Case Study 1: Patagonia – Apparel Industry

Patagonia is an outdoor clothing company that has set the pace in upholding sustainable practices. They have implemented a number of successful green initiatives such as the Common Threads Recycling Program, which encourages customers to return used garments for them to be recycled. The company also launched the Worn Wear program which promotes repair and reuse, increasing the longevity of their products. They also reduced their environmental footprint by switching to organic cotton, recycled materials, and renewable energy sources. Due to the success of these initiatives, Patagonia has been able to garner customer loyalty and strengthen its reputation as an environmentally responsible brand.

## Case Study 2: Tesla – Automotive Industry

Electric vehicle manufacturer, Tesla, has raised the bar in all ramifications when it comes to sustainable practices in the automotive industry. This is a revolutionary company that has expedited the world's transition to renewable energy through the promotion of electric transportation. Equipped with components that have minimal environmental impact, Tesla's innovative electric vehicles also have long-range capabilities and fast-charging systems that have redefined green transportation while serving as an inspiration that other auto manufacturers can emulate.

## Case Study 3: Unilever – Consumer Goods Industry

Unilever, a multinational consumer goods company, has made sustainability a core part of its business strategy. They launched the Sustainable Living Plan, focusing on reducing environmental impact and improving social welfare. Unilever set ambitious targets to achieve carbon neutrality, zero waste to landfill, and sustainable sourcing. Initiatives like the Lifebuoy handwashing campaign have positively impacted public health. Unilever's commitment to sustainability has enhanced brand reputation, increased market share, and demonstrated the business case for integrating social and environmental responsibility into operations.

### Case Study 4: IKEA - Home Furnishings Industry

IKEA, a leading home furnishings retailer, is dedicated to sustainability across its operations. They prioritize resource efficiency by using renewable energy, optimizing packaging, and promoting responsible wood sourcing. IKEA's investment in solar and wind energy has enabled them to generate more renewable energy than they consume. They also encourage customers to embrace sustainability through affordable, energy-efficient products. IKEA's sustainability initiatives have resonated with consumers, leading to increased brand loyalty, and driving the demand for sustainable home furnishings.

## Case Study 5: Google - Technology Industry

Google, a technology giant, has made significant strides in sustainability. They are committed to operating on 100% renewable energy and achieving carbon neutrality. Through energy-efficient data centers and clean energy procurement, Google has reduced its carbon footprint. They also invest in renewable energy projects, accelerating the transition to a low-carbon economy. Google's sustainability efforts align with their commitment to corporate responsibility and have positioned them as an industry leader in environmental stewardship.

## Case Study 6: Coca-Cola - Beverage Industry

Coca-Cola, one of the largest beverage companies in the world, is taking some bold steps towards being more environmentally responsible. This is evident in the company's decision to reduce water consumption in their production processes and improve water efficiency. They also replenish water in the communities where they operate. Coca-Cola is actively investing in sustainable packaging, using plant-based materials and recyclable bottles to reduce plastic waste. Their "World Without Waste" initiative is particularly inspiring, as they aim to collect and recycle one bottle or can for every one they sell by 2030. These efforts prove that they are committed to upholding sustainable environmental and circular economy principles.

## Case Study 7: Marriott International - Hospitality Industry

Marriott International, a leading hospitality company, is making giant strides in the journey towards environmental sustainability. They have introduced energy-efficient lighting, HVAC systems, and smart thermostats in their hotels to reduce energy and water consumption. Marriott is also reducing waste by implementing recycling and composting programs and cutting down on single-use plastics. Their "Serve 360: Doing Good in Every Direction" initiative is especially impressive since it emphasizes environmental sustainability, social impact, and community engagement.

## Case Study 8: Siemens - Engineering and Electronics Industry

Siemens, a global engineering and electronics firm is deeply engaged in environmental stewardship. They are on track to achieve carbon-neutrality by 2030 through their innovative green initiatives. Their products such as automation systems, smart grids, and efficient manufacturing processes contribute to energy conservation and sustainability. Siemens also supports renewable energy projects and has drastically cut their carbon emissions. Their dedication to a sustainable future sets a commendable example for other companies to follow.

## Case Study 9: Johnson & Johnson - Pharmaceutical Industry

Pharmaceutical giant, Johnson & Johnson, aims to be carbon neutral and use 100% renewable energy by 2025. They're utilizing energy-efficient technologies like LED lighting and modern HVAC systems to reduce energy usage across their facilities. They've also adopted sustainable packaging and waste reduction strategies, aligning their operations with principles of a circular economy for environmental responsibility and better public health.

## Case Study 10: Walmart - Retail Industry

Walmart, the global retail behemoth, is setting the pace for sustainability within its industry. They've made a bold pledge to operate on 100% renewable energy and eliminate waste in their operations. They're reducing greenhouse gas emissions by implementing energy-efficient solutions in their stores, distribution centers, and vehicles. Furthermore, Walmart is promoting sustainable sourcing and encouraging their suppliers to reduce their environmental impact.

## Case Study 11: Chatham University Eden Hall Campus – Education Industry

Chatham University's Eden Hall Campus stands as a remarkable case study in sustainability and innovation within the realm of hospitality and food service, housing America's first all-electric campus kitchen in the world's first fully self-sustained net-zero energy university campus. This pioneering facility employs cutting-edge technologies such as induction cooktops, electric convection ovens, and demand-controlled kitchen ventilation systems, setting it apart in energy efficiency and reducing its carbon footprint. The kitchen's design aligns with the campus's broader commitment to sustainability, serving as a living laboratory that educates students and visitors about the critical role of renewable energy and efficient design in combating climate change. Remarkably, the all-electric kitchen works in synergy with the campus's microgrid, which is primarily powered by renewable energy sources, thereby providing a holistic, eco-friendly approach to food service operations. Eden Hall Campus demonstrates how conscientious planning and innovative technology can merge to create a sustainably powered, operationally efficient, and educational environment.

## Conclusion

This chapter has provided a foundational understanding of the hospitality industry's role within the broader context of the Green Industrial Revolution. We have explored how sustainability is not merely an ethical choice but also an imperative for business success, especially as eco-conscious consumer behavior gains momentum. This chapter serves as a primer, offering insights into key trends, technologies, and challenges, all of which combine to shape the future of sustainable practices in hospitality.

As we continue through this textbook, we will delve into these topics more deeply, offering actionable strategies for navigating the complexities of sustainability in various facets of the hospitality industry. Whether you are a stakeholder, student, or someone interested in contributing to a more sustainable future, the chapters ahead will equip you with the necessary tools and knowledge to make a meaningful impact.

# Chapter 2

# Understanding the Hospitality Industry

## Introduction to the hospitality industry and its current environmental impact

The hospitality industry is a multifaceted realm that encompasses hotels, restaurants, event spaces, and various tourism services. It's an industry that not only fuels economies but also provides settings where people celebrate, relax, and connect. However, this comes at an environmental cost. The operational needs of these businesses, which involve considerable energy for heating, cooling, and lighting—as well as extensive water usage for everything from guest services to laundry and landscaping—translate into significant carbon footprints.

The industry's environmental challenges don't end with energy and water. Waste management, particularly concerning food waste in kitchens and single-use plastics, is another area requiring urgent attention. For instance, chefs and kitchen staff are often responsible for a substantial portion of a hospitality business's waste. And let's not overlook the emissions resulting from transportation needs, which form an integral part of the guest experience and logistical operations.

The silver lining here is that the sector is increasingly aware of its environmental responsibilities. Many establishments are turning to experts across various fields—from architects designing energy-efficient buildings to engineers developing smart control systems—for solutions. They are adopting more sustainable technologies, such as LED lighting and energy management systems, and are implementing water-saving solutions, some even integrating wastewater treatment into their operations. In the realm of waste management, best practices now extend to composting and reducing single-use plastics. The rising trend of locally sourced food, often directed by chefs conscious of their kitchens' impact, not only satisfies the palate but also reduces transportation-related emissions.

At the intersection of political science and sustainability, we find an increasing number of policy initiatives and community engagement programs aimed at further reducing the industry's environmental impact. These initiatives reflect a growing commitment within the hospitality industry to operate sustainably. They signal the industry's larger role in the global movement toward environmental stewardship, drawing us one step closer to realizing the goals of the Green Industrial Revolution.

## 2.1  A Multi-Dimensional Analysis for a Sustainable Future

As the hospitality industry stands at the crossroads of economic progress and environmental sustainability, understanding its operational intricacies is more important than ever. This sector, comprising hotels, resorts, restaurants, and various other services, is a cornerstone of modern economies, but it also poses significant challenges in terms of energy consumption, waste generation, and carbon emissions. This section delves into these critical areas, examining them through a multi-disciplinary lens that draws from fields as diverse as architecture, engineering, culinary arts, political science, and sustainability. By dissecting these facets, we aim to present an analytical foundation upon which the industry can build more sustainable, environmentally responsible practices. This sets the stage for a discussion on feasible green practices and technologies that could drive the hospitality sector towards a more sustainable trajectory in alignment with the emerging Green Industrial Revolution.

Now let's delve into each of three of the most pivotal concerns: energy consumption, waste generation, and carbon emissions.

## 2.1.1 Energy Consumption: A Detailed Look Through the Lens of Energy Use Intensity (EUI)

The issue of energy consumption in the hospitality industry is particularly striking when examined through the lens of Energy Use Intensity (EUI), a key metric that calculates the energy consumed per square foot per year. To illustrate the dramatic disparity, consider that a cafeteria-style kitchen has an average EUI of around 325, while a typical office building averages an EUI of just 30. This means that a commercial kitchen can be almost 11 times more energy-intensive than an office building, making it one of the most energy-consuming spaces within the built environment.

These alarming EUI figures largely arise from the constant operation of energy-intensive appliances, from ovens and stovetops to refrigerators and HVAC systems. Additionally, high-volume kitchens, such as those found in large hotels or banquet facilities, can see their EUI values rise even higher, sometimes exceeding the average by considerable margins. This energy intensity necessitates a robust strategy for energy management, which is where architects, engineers, and sustainability experts can come together to develop integrated solutions.

Understanding the EUI not only quantifies the scale of the issue but also enables more effective interventions. For example, an establishment that is aware of its high EUI can target its most energy-intensive operations or equipment for efficiency upgrades, such as installing induction cooking, advanced energy management systems, and demand control kitchen ventilation. Regular energy audits can further pinpoint inefficiencies, thereby setting actionable energy reduction goals. Thus, EUI serves as a vital tool for the hospitality industry, illuminating the path towards reducing its carbon footprint through smarter, more sustainable energy use.

## 2.1.2 Waste Generation: A Closer Examination of Excessive Waste in the Hospitality Sector

The hospitality industry is notorious for generating a significant amount of waste, a consequence of its diverse range of services which include food preparation, lodging, and events. Consider, for instance, the food waste generated from buffets, where it's not uncommon for hotels to discard large quantities of unconsumed food. Furthermore, single-use items like shampoo bottles, soap bars, and miniature toiletries provided in guest rooms often end up as waste after a single use. Events like conferences and weddings also contribute, often leaving behind not only food waste but also items like banners, printed materials, and decorations.

Another example can be found in the extensive use of single-use plastics for beverages and meals, particularly in fast-service scenarios or for room service. These include plastic straws, stirrers, and cutlery, which not only generate waste but are also significant contributors to plastic pollution. Similarly, commercial kitchens in the industry produce organic waste, including vegetable peels, expired products, and other food remnants, at a scale far larger than domestic kitchens.

The good news is that this has opened up an avenue for engineers, chefs, and sustainability experts to collaborate on innovative waste management solutions. For example, many establishments are now composting organic waste or converting used oil into biofuel. Others are implementing technological solutions like smart waste bins that can sort recyclables automatically. In addition, sustainability-driven chefs are exploring 'root-to-stem' cooking to utilize all parts of an ingredient and minimize waste.

Understanding and addressing these multiple layers of waste generation is critical for the hospitality industry's transition to sustainable operations. It's not just about waste management but also about waste prevention, requiring a multi-dimensional approach that involves technology, education, and community engagement.

## 2.1.3 Carbon Emissions: Zooming In On Hospitality's Carbon Footprint

The hospitality sector's carbon emissions are a multifaceted issue, with significant contributions stemming from diverse operational aspects. One prominent area is the energy-intensive nature of commercial kitchens, which can require constant refrigeration, inefficient cooking appliances, and hot water supplies. These operations are particularly egregious contributors to carbon emissions, especially when powered by fossil fuels. Moreover, HVAC systems in hotels, designed to provide round-the-clock comfort, contribute substantially to carbon emissions.

Another angle of excess carbon emissions is related to the supply chain. For example, if a restaurant sources its ingredients from distant locations, the transportation of these goods can substantially inflate the establishment's carbon footprint. The same can be said for hotels that import linen or furniture from far-off countries, thereby contributing to emissions from shipping and possibly even air freight.

Transportation for guests is another critical area. Hotels that provide shuttle services, for instance, contribute to emissions, particularly if these services are not optimized for efficiency or if they use older, fuel-inefficient vehicles. While air travel falls outside the direct responsibility of the hospitality industry, the sector often plays a part in promoting destinations that require long-haul flights, thereby indirectly contributing to air travel emissions.

The alarming scale of these emissions has led to collaborations among engineers, architects, and sustainability experts in the development of greener buildings, more efficient technologies, and more sustainable practices. These can range from adopting energy-efficient electrified appliances and lighting to encouraging the use of public transport or offering electric vehicle charging stations. By focusing on these aspects, the hospitality industry can significantly reduce its carbon emissions, aligning more closely with global efforts to mitigate climate change.

## 2.2  Identifying opportunities for sustainability and green practices in the hospitality sector

As the hospitality sector grapples with the pressing challenges posed by climate change, resource depletion, and a shifting consumer landscape, the need for innovative solutions has never been greater. The concept of sustainability has matured from being a niche concern to a critical business imperative. With heightened awareness among travelers, regulatory pressures, and the moral imperative to act, adopting sustainability is not just 'good-to-have' but a 'must-have' for survival and growth. The emphasis is not merely on reducing the negative impact but transforming it into a positive contribution towards environmental and social wellness. For this reason, this section delves into a multi-disciplinary approach to sustainability in hospitality, borrowing wisdom from diverse fields like technology, architecture, and social sciences. Below, we explore a range of actionable opportunities, from targeted energy efficiency to guest-centric sustainable practices, that the hospitality sector can employ to align their operations more closely with the principles of sustainability.

**Targeted Energy Efficiency**

Energy efficiency is not just a buzzword; it's a multifaceted strategy with far-reaching implications for the hospitality sector. As an industry notorious for its high energy usage the sector has a unique responsibility to lessen its environmental impact. For instance, buildings with commercial kitchens can consume 5 to 7 times more energy per square foot than other commercial buildings. In extreme cases, high-volume kitchens can even use up to 10 times more energy. Understanding Energy Use Intensity (EUI) becomes vital in this context. To put it in perspective, a cafeteria-style kitchen can have an average EUI of 325, while a typical office building has an average EUI of just 30.

The concept of 'Targeted Energy Efficiency' takes a granular approach, pinpointing specific high-impact areas for improvement within hospitality operations. An establishment aware of its high EUI can strategically target its most energy-intensive operations or equipment for efficiency upgrades. Examples of such targeted measures include the installation of induction cooking systems that are far more efficient than traditional gas systems. Building Management Systems (BMS) can offer real-time monitoring and automation features to optimize energy use across different operational areas, from guest rooms to kitchens. Demand control kitchen ventilation systems can also be employed to adapt to the specific needs of the kitchen environment, turning on and off as needed, thereby conserving energy.

Another aspect where targeted energy efficiency can make a substantial difference is in employee training and guest engagement. The staff should be educated on the importance of energy-saving measures, from something as simple as switching off unused lights to more complex tasks like operating new energy-efficient kitchen equipment. Guests too can be a part of this initiative through simple practices like using key cards that activate room electricity or opting for a digital check-in and check-out to save paper.

In summary, targeted energy efficiency is not a one-off measure but a continuous, evolving strategy. By employing advanced technologies, regular auditing, staff training, and guest participation, hospitality businesses can significantly reduce their energy consumption, thereby lowering both operational costs and environmental impact. Establishments with high Energy Use Intensity (EUI) can zero in on the most energy-consuming operations. For example, integrating advanced energy management systems, demand control kitchen ventilation, and induction cooking can significantly lower a building's EUI and thereby its carbon footprint.

## Adoption of Renewable Energy

Renewable energy adoption is more than just an environmentally conscious decision; it's a transformative strategy that has the potential to revolutionize the way the hospitality industry operates. The significance of transitioning from traditional, fossil fuel-based energy sources to renewable options like solar, wind, and geothermal energy cannot be overstated. The benefits go beyond reducing carbon emissions and extend to improving the brand image, reducing long-term operational costs, and aligning the business with global sustainability goals.

Solar energy is one of the most popular and feasible options for many establishments. Rooftop solar panels can not only provide electricity for daily operations but also have the potential to generate surplus energy that can be fed back into the grid. Moreover, solar water heating systems can be a highly efficient alternative for hot water requirements in the establishment, contributing to both energy and cost savings.

Geothermal energy is another innovative solution, particularly relevant for heating and cooling needs. Geothermal systems utilize the Earth's constant underground temperature to provide heating in the winter and cooling in the summer. These systems can be expensive to install but offer excellent long-term returns on investment, both in terms of energy savings and reduced maintenance costs.

Wind energy, while less commonly adopted due to space and logistical constraints, can be a viable option for establishments located in windy regions. Wind turbines can be installed on-site or through community wind projects to offset a part or the entirety of an establishment's electricity needs.

The adoption of renewable energy also opens doors for certification as a green or eco-friendly establishment, attracting a growing demographic of eco-conscious travelers. Additionally, many jurisdictions offer financial incentives like tax credits, grants, or rebates to businesses that invest in renewable energy installations, making the transition more economically favorable.

Importantly, renewable energy adoption also calls for smart management practices. This involves integrating renewable sources with existing systems in the most efficient way, often aided by advanced Building Management Systems (BMS) that can balance energy supply, storage, and consumption seamlessly.

In summary, the adoption of renewable energy in the hospitality industry represents a multifaceted opportunity to improve environmental sustainability, reduce long-term operational costs, and enhance brand reputation. It's an investment not just in technology but in a sustainable future.

## Data-Driven Water Conservation

Water is one of the most critical yet finite resources on the planet, and the hospitality industry is a significant consumer. As such, adopting data-driven water conservation strategies isn't merely an optional sustainability practice; it's an essential component of responsible business management. The beauty of using data-driven approaches is that they provide actionable insights into water use, allowing for targeted interventions that can yield substantial water and cost savings without compromising guest experience.

Advancements in technology have made it possible to install smart water meters that can track water usage in real-time across various departments of a hospitality establishment—be it laundry services, swimming pools, kitchens, or guest rooms. These smart meters can integrate with a centralized management system, giving administrators a detailed picture of water consumption patterns.

For instance, high-resolution data can reveal if certain times of day or specific areas within the establishment are particularly water intensive. Such data insights could lead to scheduled or sensor-based irrigation for landscapes, or they could trigger alarms for potential leaks or overuse in real-time, allowing for quick corrective action.

Low-flow fixtures are a popular water-saving feature that benefits significantly from data monitoring. While it's known that these fixtures can save water, smart meters can quantify just how effective they are, offering evidence that can be used to encourage further investment in water-saving technologies.

Data-driven strategies also enable better guest engagement in water conservation efforts. The data collected can be translated into easily understandable metrics and shared with guests, encouraging them to take part in the establishment's water-saving initiatives. This transparency not only educates guests but also enhances the establishment's reputation as a responsible and sustainable choice for travelers.

Even wastewater can be intelligently managed using data-driven approaches. Advanced filtration and treatment systems can recycle wastewater for non-potable uses, like landscape irrigation or toilet flushing. Data analytics can help optimize these systems, ensuring they operate at peak efficiency and contribute effectively to overall water conservation goals.

To supplement these efforts, hospitality establishments can also partner with local environmental agencies or NGOs, sharing data and insights to promote community-wide water conservation initiatives.

In conclusion, data-driven water conservation is not just a trend but an imperative for the modern hospitality industry. By leveraging the power of data analytics and smart technology, establishments can enact meaningful changes that have a lasting positive impact on both the environment and the bottom line.

## Smart Waste Management

Waste management is a complex challenge for the hospitality industry, which often generates significant amounts of waste ranging from food scraps and packaging to operational waste. However, the advent of smart waste management technologies is transforming how the industry handles this issue, converting a challenge into an opportunity for sustainability and even cost reduction.

Smart waste management systems employ a combination of sensor technology, data analytics, and automation to optimize waste collection and recycling. Sensors can be fitted into waste bins and containers to monitor their fill levels in real-time. This data is sent to a central management system, which can then schedule pick-ups or signal staff to empty the containers only when they are near full, thereby increasing operational efficiency.

Another benefit of smart waste management is its role in effective waste sorting. Advanced systems can now identify and separate recyclable materials, ensuring they are not sent to a landfill but instead channeled into recycling programs. For instance, smart bins can use weight sensors and cameras to identify the types of waste being deposited, automatically sorting recyclables from non-recyclables. This enhances the accuracy of recycling efforts and reduces the burden on staff to manually sort waste.

The data collected can also inform strategic decisions around waste reduction. For example, if data shows that a significant percentage of food waste is coming from a specific meal period or type of food, adjustments can be made to the menu or portion sizes. Likewise, if single-use plastics like straws and utensils make up a large portion of waste, the data serves as a compelling rationale to switch to sustainable alternatives.

Moreover, analytics from smart waste management systems can be utilized to comply with regulations and for reporting corporate social responsibility (CSR) activities. It can help the establishment identify compliance risks before they become problems and offer transparent data reporting that can enhance brand reputation.

Hospitality businesses can also integrate their smart waste management data with customer engagement platforms to inform guests about the establishment's sustainability efforts and even offer rewards for responsible waste disposal. This can create a sense of community around sustainability efforts and improve guest loyalty.

On a broader scale, smart waste management can enable hotels and other hospitality businesses to participate in or even spearhead local and global sustainability initiatives. By sharing their waste management data and success stories, they can contribute valuable insights to communal, regional, or even international waste reduction strategies.

Smart waste management represents a crucial advancement for sustainability in the hospitality sector. The combination of real-time monitoring, data analytics, and automation allows for a more strategic, efficient, and effective approach to waste management, significantly aiding the industry in its journey toward a more sustainable future.

## Holistic Sustainable Sourcing

Sustainable sourcing is not merely a trend but a necessity for a greener future, especially within the hospitality industry. Holistic sustainable sourcing goes beyond simply buying local produce or choosing suppliers with a green certification; it encompasses an integrated approach that scrutinizes every aspect of the supply chain, from farm to fork, from factory to guestroom.

The first step in this comprehensive approach is conducting a thorough audit of existing suppliers, evaluating their environmental practices, labor conditions, and overall sustainability metrics. By doing so, an establishment gains a clear understanding of the ecological and social impact of their current sourcing strategy. This forms the basis for making informed changes.

Holistic sustainable sourcing considers both the environmental and socio-economic aspects of procurement. It often involves a shift to circular economics, where products are designed to be reused or easily recycled, thereby reducing waste. For example, the hospitality industry can establish partnerships with farms that grow canola for oil, selling the oil for use in kitchens, and then collecting the refuse oil for biofuel in their operations. This creates a closed-loop system that benefits both parties while significantly reducing waste and carbon emissions. This symbiotic relationship promotes sustainability across different aspects of the supply chain, extending from food production to energy consumption.

Another important dimension is food sourcing. A holistic approach would involve not only sourcing organic or local produce but also considering the carbon footprint associated with the transportation of these goods. Seasonal menu planning is a solution that aligns with this strategy, as it allows for the inclusion of locally available, fresh produce, reducing the need for items that require long-distance transportation. Some chefs even go a step further by having their own kitchen gardens, ensuring the utmost freshness and reducing carbon emissions associated with food transportation.

Sustainability in sourcing also extends to service providers, from cleaning companies to outsourced IT services. Are they aligned with the business' sustainability goals? Do they follow eco-friendly practices? These are critical questions to ask in the selection process.

It's also essential to integrate technology to track and analyze supplier performance. Sustainability dashboards that aggregate real-time data from suppliers can provide valuable insights into how well different vendors meet sustainability goals. This data-driven approach allows for ongoing improvement and ensures accountability.

A holistic approach to sustainable sourcing also involves educating and engaging the staff. After all, they are the ones who will be implementing these changes on a daily basis. Training programs that impart the importance and benefits of sustainable sourcing can go a long way in ensuring the success of these initiatives.

Customer engagement is the final, critical element. A transparent communication strategy that informs guests about the establishment's sustainable sourcing efforts can not only educate the public but also attract a more eco-conscious clientele.

In conclusion, holistic sustainable sourcing is an all-encompassing, data-driven, and transparent approach that has the potential to significantly reduce the environmental and social impact of the hospitality industry. By applying a multi-faceted lens to procurement practices, the sector can contribute meaningfully to global sustainability goals while also enhancing brand reputation and customer loyalty.

## Green Building Design and Retrofitting

The concept of green building design and retrofitting serves as a cornerstone in the hospitality industry's journey towards sustainability. This approach not only pertains to new constructions but also addresses the vast number of existing structures that can be optimized for environmental performance. Far from being a superficial layer of "greenwashing," genuinely sustainable building design and retrofitting include a range of strategies, technologies, and practices that substantially minimize environmental impact while often delivering cost savings in the long term.

- *Foundational Elements*

The foundation of green building design starts with location and orientation. Where a building sits in relation to its natural surroundings can have significant impacts on energy use. For example, strategically placing a building to make the most out of natural light can substantially reduce the need for artificial lighting. Additionally, considering factors like local climate and wind patterns can also inform the design, enabling more efficient heating and cooling systems.

- *Energy Efficiency*

As previously mentioned, Energy Use Intensity (EUI) serves as a crucial metric for understanding a building's energy consumption. Green building design aims to minimize the EUI by incorporating features like advanced insulation, energy-efficient windows, and smart lighting systems that adjust based on occupancy and natural light. High EUI values can also guide retrofitting efforts, targeting the most energy-intensive operations or systems for upgrades such as induction cooking, advanced energy management systems, and demand control kitchen ventilation.

- *Water Conservation*

Green building design integrates water-saving technologies like low-flow toilets, -sensor-based taps, and gray water recycling systems that treat and reuse wastewater for non-potable needs like landscaping. Rainwater harvesting can provide an additional source of water, reducing dependence on municipal supplies.

- *Material Sourcing*

Sustainable building materials are another crucial aspect of green design. The use of recycled, renewable, and non-toxic materials not only reduces the building's carbon footprint but can also create a healthier indoor environment for guests and staff. Examples include bamboo flooring, recycled steel, and low-VOC paints.

- *Technological Integration*

The use of Building Management Systems (BMS) and other advanced technologies helps in real-time monitoring and management of various building functions. From controlling HVAC systems based on occupancy to managing energy consumption centrally, technology serves as the backbone for executing green building principles effectively.

- *Guest Experience*

Sustainable building features can enhance the guest experience as well. Features like natural ventilation, maximized daylight, and the use of natural materials can make spaces more comfortable and inviting, thereby contributing to guest satisfaction and overall well-being.

- *Retrofitting Existing Structures*

For older buildings, retrofitting is often the most feasible option. This can range from installing energy-efficient lighting to more complex modifications like implementing an energy management system or even structural changes to improve insulation.

- *Certification and Compliance*

Earning green building certifications such as EcoChef, LEED, or BREEAM can serve as tangible proof of a building's sustainability efforts, making it more attractive to eco-conscious guests.

In conclusion, green building design and retrofitting present a comprehensive approach to sustainability in the hospitality industry. Through the strategic use of design elements, technological solutions, and sustainable practices, these initiatives serve to significantly lower the environmental impact while also offering economic benefits in the form of energy and water savings. As consumers become increasingly aware and demanding of sustainable practices, green building design stands as an essential facet of a holistic approach to sustainability in hospitality.

## Guest-Centric Sustainable Practices

Guest-centric sustainable practices in the hospitality industry are an emerging paradigm that recognizes the role of guests in enhancing sustainability initiatives. These practices are not confined to just hotels but span across other hospitality businesses like restaurants, event venues, and travel services. The idea is to integrate sustainability into the very fabric of the guest experience, making it an inherent part of the service offered rather than a side feature. In doing so, businesses not only heighten their own eco-friendly profiles but also engage consumers in a way that encourages sustainable behavior.

- *Information and Education*

One of the foundational aspects of guest-centric sustainable practices is information dissemination and education. From digital brochures outlining a restaurant's farm-to-table initiatives to interactive displays at museums that educate visitors about energy conservation, information can be a powerful tool to involve guests in sustainability practices. Even travel agencies can contribute by providing travelers with tips on sustainable tourism or offering eco-friendly travel packages.

- *Choice Architecture*

Offering guests choices that make it easy for them to engage in sustainable practices can significantly impact behavior. For instance, a café could replace single-use items with reusable ones and clearly label bins for compost, recycling, and landfill waste. Event venues might offer electronic tickets and programs instead of paper ones, in addition to ensuring easy access to public transportation. By redesigning the "choice architecture," businesses guide guests toward making more sustainable decisions without compromising on their freedom or convenience.

- *Participatory Programs*

Many hospitality businesses are implementing participatory programs like loyalty rewards for green choices, opportunities for guests to offset their carbon footprint, or even contests that gamify conservation practices. Such initiatives foster a sense of community and shared responsibility among guests. For instance, a restaurant may offer discounts to patrons who bring their own reusable containers, or a theme park might reward guests for participating in a recycling challenge.

- *Feedback Loops*

Providing real-time or periodic feedback to guests about the positive impact of their choices can be remarkably effective. Whether it's an app that tracks the amount of plastic a guest has helped recycle during their stay at a resort or a dashboard that shows the energy saved by diners who chose a plant-based option at a restaurant, feedback mechanisms reinforce good behavior and create a more engaging, satisfying experience for the guest.

- *Customization and Personalization*

Sustainability doesn't have to be a one-size-fits-all approach. Businesses can offer customized experiences that allow guests to engage with sustainability at their own comfort level. For example, a travel agency might offer several different "shades" of green travel packages, ranging from basic to ultra-sustainable. Similarly, a spa might offer a range of eco-friendly treatments, using organic or locally-sourced products, allowing guests to choose how "green" they wish their experience to be.

In a nutshell, guest-centric sustainable practices provide a dual benefit: they allow hospitality businesses to showcase their commitment to sustainability, while also actively engaging their clientele in meaningful eco-friendly actions. By incorporating such practices, the hospitality industry can amplify its sustainability efforts and create a ripple effect that encourages broader societal change.

## Strategic Collaborations and Partnerships

Strategic collaborations and partnerships serve as critical accelerants for sustainability initiatives in the hospitality industry, extending well beyond the realm of hotels into restaurants, travel agencies, event venues, and even transportation services. By forging relationships with other stakeholders, such as local suppliers, government agencies, NGOs, and even competitors, businesses can leverage shared knowledge, resources, and influence to make more substantial strides in sustainability. These partnerships not only bring about economic synergies but also create a collective impact that individual businesses might find challenging to achieve on their own.

- *Supply Chain Partnerships*

One of the most direct ways to integrate sustainability is through supply chain collaborations. Restaurants can partner with local farms for organic produce, while airlines might collaborate with biofuel companies to reduce their carbon emissions. Event venues can source their materials from eco-friendly suppliers, thus ensuring that every aspect of their operation, from food and beverages to decorations, is sustainable. These partnerships facilitate a smoother transition to sustainable practices and often come with the added advantage of boosting local economies.

- *Community Engagement*

Collaborations with local communities can result in a more culturally and environmentally sensitive approach to hospitality. For example, a travel agency could partner with local artisans to offer workshops, thus providing tourists with an authentic experience while supporting local crafts. Adventure tourism businesses might work with local environmental organizations to educate guests about the natural habitats they explore, making sustainability an integral part of the guest experience.

- **Industry Associations and Certifications**

Partnerships with industry associations can facilitate the sharing of best practices and offer routes to various sustainability certifications. Whether it's a restaurant seeking a 'EcoChef Certification' or a cruise line working towards a 'Green Seal,' the guidance and credibility provided by industry bodies can serve as a strong incentive for both the business and the consumers choosing it.

- **Policy Influence and Advocacy**

Collaborative partnerships can extend to working with governmental bodies to advocate for sustainable policies affecting the industry. For instance, a coalition of different hospitality businesses can lobby for tax incentives for sustainable practices, making it financially more feasible for companies in the sector to adopt green technologies.

- **Consumer Partnerships**

Finally, a collaborative approach to sustainability also includes the end consumer. Businesses can develop partnerships with consumers by offering them platforms to voice their sustainability preferences, thus making them active participants in shaping the business's sustainable practices. Whether through crowdsourced initiatives to choose new eco-friendly amenities or through customer forums that discuss sustainability, businesses can make consumers a vital part of their sustainability narrative.

The preceding sections of this chapter provided a comprehensive overview of the environmental challenges and opportunities facing the hospitality industry. We delved into critical areas such as energy consumption, waste generation, and carbon emissions, highlighting the urgency for action as well as the pathways for sustainable change.

We learned that energy consumption in hospitality is particularly significant, often surpassing other types of commercial buildings. The sector's Energy Use Intensity (EUI) provides a quantifiable metric that can guide targeted energy efficiency upgrades. Waste generation, too, is a major concern, from the enormous volumes of food waste to the usage of single-use plastics. Carbon emissions serve as another focal point, generated not just from energy use but also from the entire operational ecosystem of the hospitality sector, including transportation and waste management.

The chapter then shifted its focus to the myriad opportunities available for sustainability, covering areas like targeted energy efficiency, renewable energy adoption, data-driven water conservation, and smart waste management. The idea of holistic sustainable sourcing emphasized the importance of making ethical and eco-friendly choices across the supply chain. Green building designs and retrofitting options were presented as methods for reducing the built environment's impact on natural resources. We also considered the significant role of guest-centric sustainable practices and the potential of strategic collaborations to multiply the sustainability impact.

From LED lighting and advanced building management systems to community engagement and policy advocacy, it is evident that sustainability in the hospitality sector is not a singular action but a complex, multi-faceted endeavor. It involves the active participation of stakeholders at all levels—from individual guests to global industry associations.

In conclusion, this chapter underscores that the path to sustainability is not just a responsibility but also an opportunity for the hospitality industry. Implementing the practices discussed can not only mitigate environmental impact but also offer competitive advantages, including cost savings, brand enhancement, and customer loyalty. It serves as a call to action for the industry to harness these opportunities proactively, working collaboratively towards a greener, more sustainable future.

# Chapter 3

# Green Technologies in the Hospitality Industry

## Introduction to various green technologies and their applications

As the world navigates the complexities of the emerging green industrial revolution, the hospitality industry is no exception. This sector is undergoing transformative changes through the adoption of green technologies, geared towards reducing its substantial carbon footprint, especially in the energy-intensive realm of kitchens. While traditional practices relied heavily on fossil fuels, green technologies offer sustainable alternatives that intersect with the domains of architecture, engineering, culinary arts, political science, and sustainability. This section lays the groundwork for understanding the green technologies disrupting the hospitality landscape.

# Renewable Energy Systems

Renewable energy systems, encompassing solar photovoltaic (PV) panels, wind turbines, and geothermal energy, have seen accelerated adoption across the broad spectrum of the hospitality industry—from small cafes and restaurants to large resorts and event venues. These systems offer an eco-friendly alternative to traditional fossil fuel-based energy sources. By harnessing energy from the sun, wind, or earth, these technologies contribute significantly to reducing the industry's carbon footprint. The reduced greenhouse gas emissions align not just with environmental sustainability goals but also resonate with the eco-conscious values of an increasing segment of customers, making it a win-win investment.

The installation of renewable energy systems has also been influenced by the collaborative efforts of architects and engineers who are now integrating these technologies into both new and existing building designs. For example, solar panels can be seamlessly incorporated into building layouts to maximize sun exposure, or wind turbines can be situated in optimal locations to harness wind energy most efficiently. Geothermal systems can be particularly effective for heating and cooling large facilities. Thus, renewable energy options are becoming more customizable and adaptable to the specific needs and limitations of various types of hospitality businesses.

Economically, while the initial investment in renewable energy systems can be substantial, the long-term benefits often justify the costs. Government incentives, tax breaks, and even grants are becoming increasingly available to offset initial expenses. Moreover, the operational savings in energy costs can be significant over time, making it a financially sound decision in the long run. As the hospitality industry faces growing pressure to adopt sustainable practices, renewable energy systems not only offer an effective way to decrease operational costs but also provide a competitive edge in a market that is becoming ever more focused on sustainability.

- **Smart Energy Management Systems**

Smart energy systems, such as Energy Management Systems (EMS), are revolutionizing how energy is consumed and managed across the vast expanse of the hospitality sector, including restaurants, resorts, conference centers, and even cruise ships. Utilizing a blend of automation, advanced sensors, and data analytics, EMS platforms allow for real-time monitoring and control of energy use. For example, these systems can automatically adjust lighting, HVAC systems, and kitchen appliances based on occupancy or time of day, drastically reducing energy wastage. The role of engineers and data scientists is crucial here, as they help design and interpret the analytics to create the most efficient energy use scenarios.

The introduction of smart energy systems also plays a significant role in contributing to a business's EUI. In sectors of the hospitality industry that have inherently high EUI values, such as commercial kitchens, EMS can be an absolute game-changer. By targeting the most energy-intensive operations or equipment, such as the transition to induction cooking or the implementation of demand control kitchen ventilation, establishments can drastically reduce their EUI, achieving both financial and environmental benefits.

In terms of economics, smart energy systems often lead to significant reductions in operational costs, with the added advantage of being good for the planet—a compelling selling point for eco-conscious consumers. While the upfront cost of implementing these systems can be a barrier, the long-term cost benefits often outweigh the initial investment, especially when considering potential tax incentives or grants for adopting green technologies. These systems not only make economic sense but also position the adopting businesses as industry leaders in sustainability, which is increasingly becoming a differentiator in the competitive hospitality market.

- **Energy-Efficient Lighting and Smart Building Automation**

The transition to energy-efficient lighting solutions like LED (Light Emitting Diodes) is more than just a trend; it's a necessity for the modern hospitality industry, encompassing hotels, restaurants, event venues, and more. Unlike traditional incandescent or fluorescent lighting, LEDs consume significantly less electricity, put off less heat, and have a much longer lifespan, leading to both cost savings and a reduced carbon footprint. Architects often work in conjunction with lighting designers to optimize natural lighting and integrate LEDs in a way that enhances the aesthetic appeal of a space while minimizing energy consumption.

Smart Building Automation takes energy efficiency a step further by integrating various systems such as lighting, heating, ventilation, and air conditioning (HVAC), and even guest services into a centralized control platform. With sensors and data analytics, this centralized system can intelligently adjust energy usage according to different variables such as occupancy, outdoor temperature, and time of day. For instance, in a high-efficiency electric commercial kitchen, smart building automation can control the timing and intensity of lighting, HVAC, and even cooking equipment to ensure that energy is used only when necessary maximizing the efficiency and thus increasing financial savings.

Both energy-efficient lighting and smart building automation offer dual benefits: cost reduction and environmental responsibility. While the initial investment in these technologies may be relatively high, the long-term savings in energy costs are substantial. Moreover, these green initiatives resonate well with an increasingly eco-conscious customer base, enhancing a business's reputation and competitive edge. These solutions offer a practical pathway for the hospitality industry to not only comply with growing regulatory pressures but also to actively participate in the broader global movement toward sustainability.

- **Holistic Water Management**

Water is one of the most crucial yet often overlooked resources in the hospitality industry, impacting a range of businesses from hotels and restaurants to resorts and conference centers. Many establishments are adopting holistic water management systems that go beyond simple conservation techniques like low-flow fixtures or sensor-operated faucets. These comprehensive systems employ advanced sensors, data analytics, and automation to monitor water usage in real-time. For instance, advanced irrigation systems equipped with moisture sensors can automatically adjust watering schedules based on soil conditions and weather forecasts, thus ensuring that not a drop is wasted.

The hospitality sector is also exploring innovative water recycling and reuse methods. Greywater—water that has been used for washing dishes, showering, or laundry—can be treated and reused for non-potable purposes like flushing toilets or landscape irrigation.

This cyclical approach to water management not only reduces the demand for fresh water but also lessens the volume of wastewater discharged into the environment. Chefs and kitchen managers play a role here too; using water-efficient appliances and practices in their kitchens can drastically reduce water consumption, an essential step given the high-water usage of many commercial kitchens.

Taking a holistic approach to water management does more than just benefit the environment; it also has a direct impact on the bottom line and can significantly reduce operational costs. Furthermore, water sustainability initiatives often appeal to the eco-conscious consumer, enhancing the establishment's reputation and brand image. In summary, holistic water management is not just an environmental imperative but a strategic asset that can set a hospitality business apart in an increasingly competitive and resource-conscious world.

- **Waste Management and Sustainable Building Design**

The waste generated by the hospitality industry can be staggering, with everything from single-use plastics and food waste to electronic waste and general consumables contributing to the problem. Today, savvy hospitality businesses are investing in smart waste management systems that do much more than segregate recyclables from non-recyclables. These systems can include technologies like food waste digesters, which break down organic waste on-site, reducing the volume and associated costs of disposal. There are also intelligent waste bins equipped with sensors to monitor fullness levels, optimizing the collection schedule, and reducing carbon emissions from collection vehicles. By using these technologies, the industry not only lessens its environmental impact but also can convert waste into resources like compost or even energy.

Sustainable building design complements these waste management efforts, and its adoption has grown beyond just hotels to include restaurants, resorts, and conference centers. Green building techniques focus on energy-efficient systems, but they also use materials that are sustainable and sourced responsibly. More establishments are looking to achieve certifications like EcoChef, which sets industry standards for environmentally responsible kitchens and LEED (Leadership in Energy and Environmental Design), which sets industry standards for environmentally responsible construction. Building designs now often incorporate features such as green roofs, natural lighting, and advanced HVAC systems that contribute to overall sustainability.

The integration of smart waste management and sustainable building design serves as a multi-pronged approach to sustainability that has significant economic and social benefits. Reducing waste and using sustainable materials can result in substantial cost savings over time. Simultaneously, these practices fulfill the growing consumer demand for eco-friendly establishments, thereby enhancing brand reputation and customer loyalty. This dual focus on waste management and sustainable design is rapidly becoming not just a trend but a standard best practice in the expansive field of hospitality.

- **Efficient Electrified Commercial Cooking Equipment**

The traditional gas-powered kitchen is undergoing a green transformation, driven by the adoption of efficient electrified cooking equipment. This trend is spreading across the broad spectrum of the hospitality industry, from restaurants and cafes to hotels and event spaces. One prime example is induction cooking technology, which uses electromagnetic fields to heat cookware directly, improving efficiency and reducing energy waste. Unlike conventional gas stoves that lose a significant amount of heat to the surrounding environment, induction cooktops ensure that more energy goes into cooking the food, reducing overall energy consumption and heat emissions.

Combi ovens are another energy-efficient and versatile addition to modern commercial kitchens. These ovens combine convection cooking, steam cooking, and a combination of both, offering more control over cooking conditions and thus reducing energy consumption. They also often have energy-saving modes and pre-programmable settings to optimize their efficiency further. Such features make them highly adaptable and efficient, allowing chefs to prepare a variety of dishes using less water, energy, and time, thereby reducing the overall carbon footprint of the kitchen while maximizing its throughput.

In addition to these cooking innovations, Demand-Controlled Kitchen Ventilation (DCKV) systems are revolutionizing how commercial kitchens manage their ventilation needs. Unlike traditional ventilation systems that operate at a constant rate, DCKVs use sensors to detect heat and vapors, adjusting fan speeds accordingly. This dynamic adjustment optimizes energy usage and improves air quality, reducing both operational costs and carbon emissions.

By investing in these modern, efficient cooking technologies, hospitality businesses can significantly reduce their energy consumption and environmental impact. This shift is not just beneficial for the planet but also holds a compelling business case. Lower energy bills, potential tax incentives for green technology adoption, and increased appeal to eco-conscious consumers make these investments worthwhile. In the grand scheme of things, efficient electrified commercial cooking equipment is shaping up to be an integral component in the sustainability playbook of the hospitality industry.

By integrating these green technologies, the hospitality industry does more than just limit its environmental impact. It also lowers operational costs, attracts a growing segment of eco-conscious patrons, and stays competitive in an ever-evolving market. This symbiosis between green technologies and sustainable practices sets the stage for a more sustainable and economically viable future in hospitality.

## 3.2 Examining the current technology landscape in the hospitality industry

In an age marked by growing environmental concerns and a collective push toward sustainability, the hospitality industry finds itself at a crucial juncture. Once primarily focused on guest satisfaction and operational efficiency, businesses across the sector—from local eateries to international resort chains—are increasingly integrating green technologies and sustainable practices into their operational DNA. This evolution is not merely a nod to global eco-friendly trends but a substantive commitment to lower environmental footprints while enhancing customer experience.

The urgency to adapt is fueled by a confluence of factors, including regulatory pressures, consumer demand for eco-conscious options, and the practical benefits of long-term cost savings. This dynamic environment creates a compelling case for businesses in the hospitality industry to rethink their approach to resource management, construction, waste disposal, and even food sourcing. As we delve into the emerging green tech landscape in this sector, we'll explore how the marriage of technology and sustainability is setting the stage for a greener, more responsible hospitality industry.

1. **Advanced Energy Solutions in the Hospitality Industry:**

The hospitality industry is pushing the boundaries of what's possible with advanced energy solutions, making a decisive shift from traditional fossil fuel-powered systems to more sustainable options. One noteworthy trend is the incorporation of specialized commercial kitchen technologies like induction cooktops, combi ovens, and Demand-Controlled Kitchen Ventilation (DCKV) systems. These technologies are not only energy-efficient but also offer enhanced performance and safety. Induction cooktops, for instance, use electromagnetic fields to directly heat cookware, thereby reducing heat loss and conserving energy. Combi ovens combine convection and steam cooking, allowing chefs to optimize cooking times and temperatures, resulting in reduced energy consumption.

Implementing smart energy management systems (EMS) is another leap forward. These systems use sensors, analytics, and automation to manage a facility's energy usage dynamically. Whether it's adjusting the HVAC system in response to occupancy levels or optimizing lighting based on natural daylight availability, EMS enables a more efficient use of energy resources. These systems work around the clock and can adapt to various conditions such as weather or time of day, ensuring that energy consumption is as efficient as possible.

The strategic adoption of these advanced energy solutions not only substantially lowers utility bills but also adds significant value to the customer experience. The modern, eco-conscious consumer often seeks establishments committed to sustainability, willing to patronize those businesses making genuine efforts to reduce their environmental footprint. Therefore, advanced energy solutions are not just an operational upgrade; they are fast becoming a competitive differentiator in the ever-evolving hospitality industry.

2. **Holistic Water Management:**

Water is an invaluable resource in the hospitality industry, used in everything from cleaning and laundry to food preparation and landscape maintenance. Given the increasing scarcity of freshwater, holistic water management solutions have become imperative. Businesses are adopting a range of technologies and practices aimed at not just reducing water usage but optimizing the entire water cycle. Smart irrigation systems, for example, use weather forecasts and soil moisture levels to determine the exact amount of water needed for landscapes, thereby preventing overwatering. Inside buildings, sensor-controlled faucets, low-flow toilets, and water-efficient laundry systems contribute significantly to water conservation.

Another dimension of holistic water management is the treatment and recycling of wastewater. On-site treatment facilities can convert wastewater into reusable water for non-potable purposes like flushing toilets or irrigation. Some establishments go even further by adopting greywater systems that repurpose lightly used water from sinks and showers for similar applications. These measures not only reduce the demand for freshwater but also lower the burden on municipal wastewater treatment plants.

Incorporating these holistic water solutions serves dual purposes: it substantially decreases operational costs and aligns the business with growing consumer demand for environmental responsibility. As sustainability becomes a key decision-making factor for consumers, effective water management is becoming a business imperative, offering a competitive edge in the hospitality sector. By embracing holistic approaches to water management, the industry not only contributes to global conservation efforts but also enhances its own long-term sustainability.

3. **Innovative Waste Solutions:**

Waste management has always been a challenging issue for the hospitality industry, which traditionally produces significant amounts of organic waste, packaging, and disposable items. Recent technological innovations are offering smarter solutions that go beyond the standard practices of recycling and composting. Food waste digesters, for instance, can break down organic waste on-site, converting it into water or a nutrient-rich sludge that can be used for landscaping. Smart waste bins equipped with sensors can indicate when they are full, optimizing collection routes and reducing the frequency and cost of waste collection.

Another significant innovation is the use of block chain and Internet of Things (IoT) technologies for supply chain management. These technologies make it possible to trace the lifecycle of products and materials with great accuracy. This data-driven approach aids in identifying wasteful steps in the supply chain and allows for more informed decisions on reducing waste generation at the source. It also enables better sorting and categorization of waste, making recycling and reuse more effective.

Incorporating these innovative waste solutions is not just an environmental imperative but also a smart business move. Cost savings emerge from reduced waste collection fees, less expenditure on waste disposal, and even potential revenue streams from selling recyclable materials or compost. More importantly, these initiatives position a hospitality business as a responsible, sustainable brand, which is increasingly becoming a differentiator in a competitive market.

## 4. Sustainable Food and Beverage Practices:

The global trend toward sustainability has made its way into the kitchens and dining rooms of the hospitality industry, driving a transformation in how food and beverages are sourced, prepared, and served. Local and organic sourcing is becoming the norm rather than the exception, as businesses align their procurement strategies with the principles of sustainability. Farm-to-table initiatives are gaining momentum, shortening the supply chain, and reducing the carbon footprint associated with transporting food. Likewise, more establishments are offering plant-based menu options, not only catering to dietary preferences but also acknowledging the lower environmental impact of plant-based foods.

Waste reduction in food service operations is another area where innovative approaches are making a difference. Strategies such as portion control, menu engineering to optimize ingredient usage, and donation programs to distribute unsold but still edible food are gaining traction. These strategies not only cut down on waste but also make economic sense by reducing disposal costs and sometimes even earning tax benefits for donations. Some establishments are going a step further by utilizing food waste for composting or as a feedstock for bioenergy, turning a problem into a resource.

Investing in sustainable food and beverage practices has several benefits for the hospitality sector. Aside from the positive environmental impacts, such as reduced carbon footprint and less waste, these practices often resonate well with consumers, who are increasingly making choices based on sustainability criteria. Adopting sustainable food and beverage practices can therefore not only save costs in the long term but can also serve as a unique selling proposition, enhancing brand value and customer loyalty.

5. **Green Construction and Certification**:

Green construction methods and materials have become a focal point for the hospitality industry as it seeks to align its practices with broader sustainability goals. Businesses ranging from hotels to restaurants and conference centers are increasingly incorporating energy-efficient designs, low-impact materials, and water-saving technologies into their construction or retrofitting projects. These projects often prioritize features like natural light, improved insulation, and advanced HVAC systems to reduce energy consumption. Furthermore, materials such as bamboo, reclaimed wood, and recycled steel are being used in place of traditional building materials, lowering the environmental impact of construction projects.

The shift toward sustainable construction has been further facilitated by the availability of various green building certifications, such as LEED (Leadership in Energy and Environmental Design),

WELL, and EcoChef. These certifications serve as industry benchmarks for sustainability, guiding architects, engineers, and owners through the process of planning and building eco-friendly structures. Achieving such certification not only underscores a commitment to sustainability but also often brings financial benefits in the form of tax incentives, lower operating costs, and increased property value.

For businesses in the hospitality sector, green construction and certification offer a win-win scenario: operational cost savings alongside a strong statement of environmental responsibility. As consumers become more eco-conscious, having a green building certification becomes a significant competitive advantage. It signals to guests and stakeholders that the business is committed to sustainability, which can be a decisive factor in choice and loyalty, thereby creating a ripple effect that benefits both the environment and the bottom line.

This comprehensive embrace of green technologies and practices represents a pivotal moment for the hospitality industry. The sector is proving that it's possible to align good business sense with good environmental stewardship. As we move further into the era of the green industrial revolution, the integration of these technologies and practices will not just be an option but an imperative for staying competitive and relevant.

## 3.3 Energy-efficient solutions: renewable energy sources, energy management systems, and smart grids

In today's landscape, a host of energy-efficient solutions have been innovated to cater to various sectors, and the hospitality industry is no exception. These solutions are not merely about using less energy; they aim to create more efficient energy ecosystems that integrate renewable energy sources, intelligent energy management systems, and cutting-edge grid technologies.

Renewable energy platforms, including solar, wind, and geothermal systems, have revolutionized the way energy is generated and used across hospitality businesses—from hotels and restaurants to wellness centers and entertainment venues. These renewable sources generate clean energy, significantly reducing greenhouse gas emissions and the industry's reliance on fossil fuels. Not only do they mitigate climate impact, but they also provide a long-term, sustainable approach to energy. For instance, solar arrays can be installed on rooftops to power an entire venue, while geothermal systems can provide efficient heating and cooling solutions, reducing both operational costs and carbon footprints.

The utilization of Smart Energy Management Systems (SEMS) is another transformative aspect of energy-efficient solutions. These systems go far beyond traditional energy monitoring, offering real-time tracking and automation capabilities. Through advanced sensors and analytics, SEMS can manage various aspects of energy consumption, such as HVAC settings, lighting, and even kitchen appliances, dynamically adjusting them based on occupancy or time of day. By implementing SEMS, hospitality businesses can significantly reduce energy wastage and costs while also making data-driven decisions that further sustainability goals.

The role of intelligent grids, or smart grids, is often underestimated in creating a holistic, energy-efficient environment. These grids integrate renewable energy systems and allow for real-time data exchange, enhancing electricity distribution, and utilization. They also manage load balancing and demand response more effectively, contributing to an overall more reliable and sustainable energy infrastructure. Smart grids make it easier for hospitality businesses to adopt renewable energies, automate energy savings, and even sell excess energy back to the grid, offering both environmental and economic benefits.

In summary, the adoption of these comprehensive energy-efficient solutions can be a game-changer for the hospitality sector. Not only do they significantly reduce operational costs and the industry's environmental impact, but they also cater to a growing market of eco-conscious consumers. Implementing these technologies results in a win-win scenario—boosting sustainability while enhancing operational and financial performance, thereby aligning with the ethical and economic imperatives of the modern world.

## 3.4 Waste reduction and recycling technologies

The hospitality industry, which encompasses a broad range of businesses from restaurants to event venues, is notoriously a significant generator of waste. Nonetheless, new technologies and management strategies offer promising ways to mitigate this environmental toll. From the kitchen to the guest rooms to the corporate office, holistic waste management is an imperative for any establishment aiming to be both profitable and sustainable.

One often underemphasized but impactful area is intelligent inventory management, which helps to avoid overstocking and thereby minimize spoilage—especially crucial for businesses like restaurants where food waste is a significant concern. Equipped with advanced analytics and real-time tracking, modern inventory systems can predict demand and suggest restocking schedules, effectively reducing waste and saving costs. In addition, chefs and foodservice managers are adopting strategies like nose-to-tail or root-to-stem cooking to use all parts of ingredients and thus minimize waste, a practice that combines culinary innovation with sustainability.

Another key element in modern waste management is innovative packaging. From biodegradable takeaway containers to reusable glass bottles for beverages, hospitality businesses are rethinking packaging with sustainability in mind. Packaging innovations not only reduce the volume of waste but also address consumer demands for environmentally friendly practices.

Recycling technologies have come a long way from mere sorting and disposing. Advanced systems are now capable of mechanical sorting, composting, and even transforming waste into energy through anaerobic digestion or waste-to-energy technologies. These approaches not only divert waste from landfills but also create a circular economy where waste is viewed as a resource to be reused or transformed. Implementing such technologies can be a selling point for eco-conscious customers and can contribute to a company's green credentials.

In conclusion, implementing smart waste management technologies is not just an ethical choice but a strategic one for the modern hospitality industry. It aligns with growing customer demand for sustainability and contributes to building a brand that stands for environmental stewardship. The advent of advanced technologies for inventory management, waste reduction, and recycling enables the industry to operate more sustainably, reinforcing both its bottom line and its commitment to a greener future.

## 3.5 Water conservation and management solutions

Water is an indispensable resource in the hospitality industry, not just in hotels but also in restaurants, event venues, and spas, among others. With high consumption rates in kitchens, bathrooms, outdoor spaces, and other amenities, the need for judicious water use is pressing. This has prompted a shift toward water conservation strategies that extend beyond basic efficiency to include smart technologies and guest engagement.

Water-efficient fixtures are a staple in modern hospitality businesses. Whether it's low-flow faucets in guest rooms or sensor-based flush systems in public restrooms at entertainment venues, these fixtures dramatically decrease water usage without affecting operational effectiveness or guest satisfaction. Another crucial aspect within kitchens is optimizing water-intensive processes like dishwashing; by using water-efficient dishwashers, establishments can cut down on both water and energy use significantly. Smart irrigation is also redefining landscape management across hospitality sub-sectors. Using real-time weather data and soil moisture sensors, these systems automatically adjust water schedules, thus ensuring that outdoor spaces are watered efficiently and responsibly.

The notion of smart water management is gaining traction with practices such as rainwater harvesting and greywater recycling. For instance, rainwater collected can be purified and used for non-potable applications like flushing toilets or irrigating green spaces. Similarly, greywater systems treat water from kitchens, showers, and laundry, repurposing it for secondary uses like landscape irrigation or cooling systems. This approach not only conserves fresh water but also reduces the load on municipal water treatment facilities. In addition, proactive measures like leak detection can offer dual benefits of conserving water and averting property damage, thus saving on repair costs.

In today's competitive market, consumers are more environmentally conscious than ever before, extending their preferences for sustainability even to the places where they dine or seek entertainment. Therefore, including guests in water conservation efforts—like signage encouraging minimal water use in restaurant restrooms or linen reuse programs in boutique bed-and-breakfasts—can be a win-win, both reducing consumption and elevating brand reputation. Moreover, the financial benefits of reducing water usage can be substantial over time, allowing businesses to invest in other eco-friendly initiatives. To sum it up, holistic water management is more than a trend; it's a comprehensive approach that combines technology, operational changes, and consumer education to make a meaningful impact. By embracing these multi-faceted strategies, the hospitality industry can play a significant role in fostering a more water-efficient and sustainable future.

## 3.6 Advantages and challenges of adopting green technologies in the hospitality sector

The integration of green technologies in the hospitality sector, which includes restaurants, event venues, and wellness centers, in addition to hotels, is a nuanced endeavor. While the advantages are manifold, there are unique challenges that establishments must navigate. This comprehensive perspective will equip business operators with the tools they need to implement sustainable practices effectively.

## Advantages:

**1.** *Operational Cost Savings*: In the hospitality industry, operational costs such as energy, water, and waste management can quickly accumulate, making them significant budgetary considerations. Green technologies offer a tangible solution to this financial burden by optimizing resource usage across various departments, including kitchens, guest amenities, and general facility management. For example, installing energy-efficient appliances in restaurant kitchens can dramatically reduce electricity bills, while implementing water-saving fixtures in restrooms and cooking areas helps minimize water expenses. Smart lighting systems equipped with motion sensors can ensure that electricity is consumed only when necessary, reducing costs without compromising guest comfort. Moreover, adopting waste-sorting and recycling systems can lead to fewer waste removal fees. Collectively, these sustainable technologies offer a win-win scenario: they lessen environmental impact while also providing measurable cost savings that improve an establishment's bottom line.

**2.** *Strengthened Brand Equity*: Adopting green technologies in the hospitality sector substantially strengthens brand equity by aligning the business with the increasingly prevalent values of sustainability and environmental responsibility. Today's consumers, more educated and concerned about ecological issues, are actively seeking out establishments that share their commitment to reducing environmental impact. By integrating sustainable practices into everyday operations—from eco-friendly kitchen practices to waste management and energy conservation—hospitality businesses not only garner trust and loyalty among existing customers but also attract a growing demographic of environmentally-conscious patrons. Positive online reviews and word-of-mouth, generated by satisfied, eco-aware guests, can significantly elevate a brand's reputation, making it a leader in sustainable hospitality and thereby giving it a competitive edge in an increasingly crowded market.

**3.** *Regulatory Benefits:* Incorporating green technologies in the hospitality industry provides distinct regulatory benefits by helping businesses meet and exceed evolving environmental laws and standards. As governments worldwide become more stringent in enforcing eco-friendly regulations, businesses that proactively adopt sustainable practices are less likely to face legal repercussions, such as fines or sanctions. Moreover, some jurisdictions offer incentives like tax breaks or grants for enterprises that demonstrate exceptional environmental stewardship, thereby not only mitigating the risk of regulatory non-compliance but also offering potential financial advantages. Being ahead of the curve in adopting green technologies can prepare businesses for future changes in regulations, making the transition less disruptive and costly when new environmental laws inevitably come into effect.

**4.** *Resource Optimization*: Resource optimization is a compelling advantage of adopting green technologies in the hospitality sector, especially in areas like energy, water, and waste management. By leveraging technologies such as energy-efficient appliances, water-saving fixtures, and intelligent waste sorting systems, businesses can significantly reduce their consumption of natural resources. For instance, smart kitchens can employ IoT-enabled devices to monitor energy usage, reduce food waste, and streamline operations. Similarly, the use of water-efficient fixtures and smart irrigation systems can drastically reduce water usage, which is particularly crucial in areas prone to drought or water scarcity. Through these technologies, establishments not only lessen their environmental impact but also realize cost savings by reducing the amounts of resources needed for daily operations.

**5.** *Catalyst for Innovation*: The adoption of green technologies serves as a catalyst for innovation in the hospitality sector, pushing the industry towards a more sustainable future. As businesses integrate cutting-edge solutions like renewable energy systems, waste-to-energy converters, or AI-powered energy management systems, they inadvertently drive demand for further technological advancements tailored for sustainable practices. This creates a virtuous cycle where the industry's needs spur technology developers to innovate, resulting in increasingly efficient and effective green solutions. In turn, this innovation allows the sector to address environmental challenges more robustly and enables businesses to stay ahead of consumer expectations and regulatory requirements.

**6.** *Positive Community Engagement*: Implementing green technologies in the hospitality sector not only minimizes environmental impact but also fosters positive engagement with the local community. When a business champions sustainability, it often gains favorable publicity and increased trust among community members. This can manifest in the form of partnerships with local environmental organizations, participation in community-driven eco-projects, or even educational programs that aim to raise awareness about sustainability. By proactively contributing to community well-being and environmental conservation, a business not only bolsters its own reputation but also elevates the community's view of the entire hospitality industry as a committed steward of sustainable practices.

**7. *Consumer Loyalty*:** Embracing green technologies and sustainable practices in the hospitality sector can significantly boost consumer loyalty. Today's travelers are increasingly environmentally conscious and are more likely to return to, and recommend, establishments that demonstrate a commitment to sustainability. Whether it's through energy-efficient accommodations, waste-reduction programs, or locally sourced food in restaurants, these eco-friendly features become key differentiators that attract a dedicated customer base. Over time, this loyalty not only drives repeat business but also amplifies positive word-of-mouth, thereby creating a virtuous cycle of customer retention and new customer acquisition all centered around sustainable practices.

Challenges:

**1. *Initial Capital Outlay*:** The initial capital outlay required for implementing green technologies in the hospitality sector can be substantial, especially for smaller establishments with limited budgets. Businesses may need to invest in energy-efficient lighting systems, smart HVAC systems, water-saving fixtures, and even more extensive retrofits to integrate renewable energy sources. However, this upfront investment should be viewed as a long-term asset that pays dividends over time. The operational savings achieved through reduced utility bills, coupled with enhanced customer loyalty and potential tax incentives or grants for eco-friendly initiatives, often results in a favorable return on investment, making the initial capital outlay a strategic investment in the establishment's sustainable and financial future.

**2. *Technical Barriers*:** The technical barriers to adopting green technologies in the hospitality sector can be formidable, especially for establishments without a dedicated in-house team versed in sustainable technology. The complexity of integrating new systems like smart energy management, water conservation fixtures, or waste recycling solutions often requires specialized knowledge and can disrupt regular operations temporarily. However, these technical challenges are surmountable and often lead to operational efficiencies and innovations. By partnering with experts in the field or investing in staff training, businesses can not only overcome these barriers but also gain a competitive edge by staying ahead of the curve in technological advancements, thus reaping the long-term benefits of being pioneers in sustainable practices.

**3.** *Consumer Misconceptions*: Consumer misconceptions can pose a challenge when implementing green technologies in the hospitality sector. Some guests may perceive sustainable practices as compromises on luxury, comfort, or quality of service. They might erroneously equate water-saving fixtures or energy-efficient lighting with a less-than-premium experience. However, these misconceptions offer a valuable opportunity for education and engagement. By effectively communicating the benefits and the negligible impact on guest experience, businesses can not only correct these misunderstandings but also elevate their brand as thought leaders in sustainable hospitality. This, in turn, can attract a growing segment of eco-conscious consumers who appreciate and seek out responsible businesses.

**4.** *Knowledge Gaps*: Knowledge gaps can be a significant hurdle when it comes to the adoption of green technologies in the hospitality industry. Lack of awareness or understanding of the available technologies, their benefits, and how to implement them can deter businesses from making sustainable choices. Staff may be unfamiliar with new systems, and management might be hesitant due to uncertainties regarding return on investment or operational impact. However, these gaps are also an invitation for continuous learning and development. Training programs, workshops, and collaborations with technology providers can fill these knowledge voids, turning the challenge into an opportunity for staff empowerment and organizational growth. As teams become more knowledgeable, they are better equipped to implement sustainable practices efficiently, thereby enhancing both environmental stewardship and business competitiveness.

5. *Retrofitting Woes*: Retrofitting existing buildings with green technologies can be a complicated endeavor, presenting logistical, structural, and financial challenges. The integration of new systems may disrupt current operations and necessitate modifications to existing infrastructure, which can be costly and time-consuming. However, these retrofitting efforts can be viewed as long-term investments in the property's value and operational efficiency. When successfully implemented, they can lead to significant energy savings, enhanced guest satisfaction due to greener amenities, and compliance with environmental regulations, thus positioning the business as a leader in sustainable hospitality. This transformative process can turn older buildings into modern, eco-friendly establishments that meet the demands of today's conscientious consumer.

6. *Legislative Constraints*: Navigating the diverse and sometimes stringent legislative landscape can be a significant hurdle when adopting green technologies in the hospitality sector. Different jurisdictions have various standards and requirements that can restrict the types of technologies that can be deployed or may necessitate specific permits and approvals, which can prolong implementation timelines and add to initial costs. However, these regulations often come with government incentives, grants, or tax

breaks designed to encourage sustainable practices. By aligning their operations with these legislative frameworks, businesses not only ensure compliance but also position themselves to take advantage of financial incentives, thereby offsetting some of the initial investment and operational costs. Moreover, regulatory alignment strengthens a brand's reputation for responsible business practices, appealing to an increasingly eco-conscious clientele.

## Navigating Challenges

Navigating the multifaceted challenges of adopting green technologies requires a comprehensive and forward-thinking approach. Overcoming obstacles like initial capital outlays, technical complexities, and legislative constraints demands not only financial investment but also a commitment to staff training, customer education, and possibly even lobbying for favorable regulations. One effective strategy is to engage in industry partnerships and collaborations, which can reduce costs, pool resources, and share knowledge and best practices. Participating in sustainability-focused consortia or industry groups can provide valuable insights and support. Moreover, leveraging public and private grants, tax incentives, and other financial mechanisms can offset some of the initial investment hurdles. Engaging in a transparent dialogue with customers, employees, and stakeholders can also facilitate a smoother transition, helping to clarify misconceptions and build a community of support around sustainability initiatives. Therefore, while the challenges are numerous, a well-executed strategy encompassing financial planning, stakeholder engagement, and continuous learning can not only mitigate these challenges but also turn them into opportunities for innovation and long-term success.

## Conclusion

Chapter 3 delved into the critical considerations for implementing sustainability in the hospitality industry, focusing on water conservation, the adoption of green technologies, and both the benefits and challenges entailed. Through practical solutions such as low-flow fixtures, smart irrigation, and greywater systems, businesses can achieve notable water and energy savings while reducing their environmental footprint. Green technologies, while requiring initial investment and adaptation, offer long-term rewards including cost savings, brand enhancement, regulatory compliance, and consumer loyalty. By actively navigating the challenges of initial costs, technical complexities, and regulatory constraints, hospitality establishments can not only make significant strides in sustainability but also gain a competitive edge in an increasingly eco-conscious market. Overall, the chapter underscores that embracing sustainability is not just an ethical choice but a strategic imperative for long-term success in the hospitality industry.

# CHAPTER 4

# COMPARING GREEN TECHNOLOGIES TO GAS COUNTERPARTS

The debate over green technologies and their gas counterparts has been going on for years. With new advances in technology, it can be difficult to know which option is the best for your needs. we'll be discussing each type of technology to help you make an informed decision when it comes to your energy sources. By the end of this you'll have a better understanding of which technology is right for you and your needs.

## 4.1 Comparative analysis of traditional gas technologies versus greener alternatives

In the swiftly evolving landscape of the hospitality industry, sustainability has emerged as a focal point, drawing attention not only from industry experts but also from a diverse set of stakeholders such as architects, engineers, chefs, policy makers, and sustainability experts. The kitchen, being a significant contributor to the carbon footprint of hospitality businesses, is an area under intense scrutiny. As industries globally are riding the wave of the green industrial revolution, it becomes essential to analyze the viability, efficiency, and impact of traditional gas technologies against their greener alternatives within the hospitality sector.

This section aims to provide a comprehensive comparative analysis between traditional gas technologies and contemporary greener alternatives, focusing on five critical dimensions: environmental impact, efficiency, resource dependency, operational costs, and innovation potential. We delve into these areas to offer a multi-faceted perspective that synthesizes insights from various industries. This analysis serves as a foundation for hospitality businesses looking to make informed decisions for a sustainable future, balancing the practicalities of cost and efficiency with the urgent imperatives of environmental stewardship.

## Environmental Impact

In the realm of environmental impact, traditional gas technologies and their greener alternatives stand in stark contrast. Gas-powered systems like boilers and generators are known culprits for air pollution and greenhouse gas emissions. Specifically, these technologies emit carbon dioxide ($CO_2$), nitrogen oxides ($NOx$), and sulfur dioxide ($SO_2$), which are notorious for their contributions to climate change and air quality degradation. Engineers and sustainability experts alike point out that such emissions have long-lasting, detrimental impacts on both local ecosystems and the global climate, presenting a challenge that the hospitality industry can't afford to ignore.

In contrast, greener technologies such as wind, solar, and geothermal energy systems produce negligible, if any, direct emissions. Architects designing eco-friendly hospitality spaces now prioritize integrating these renewable technologies to not only reduce carbon footprint but also improve the overall air quality. These greener alternatives do not contribute to the release of toxic pollutants, thereby mitigating climate change impacts and enhancing the quality of air. Thus, from an environmental standpoint, greener technologies offer a substantially more sustainable and responsible path for the hospitality industry to follow, especially when one considers the long-term consequences for planetary health.

## Efficiency

When considering efficiency, gas and electric technologies each present unique operational and financial attributes. Gas-powered kitchen stoves, historically preferred over coal since the early 1900s, generally showcase laboratory efficiency rates between 30%-40%. However, under the expertise of a seasoned chef, this efficiency can sometimes dip to between 10%-20%. Despite their immediate heat production, these stoves grapple withenergy losses during transmission and the varying costs of natural gas, influenced by ever-shifting market dynamics. Thus, culinary professionals and finance experts must weigh not only the direct cooking efficiency but also the overarching landscape of operational expenses and energy wastage.

Conversely, modern electric solutions like induction cooktops consistently achieve efficiency levels between 80%-90%+, maintaining this efficiency even in real-world settings. Utilizing electromagnetic fields, these cooktops heat cookware directly, ensuring rapid and even cooking. The stellar efficiency of induction stoves has multiple operational advantages: they emit less ambient heat, which in turn reduces kitchen cooling expenses; they cook faster, boosting guest turnover rates; and their ease of cleaning not only shortens cleanup times but also minimizes the use of harsh cleaning agents, presenting additional savings. Moreover, they are more water-efficient, leading to further cost reductions. While the initial investment in such technologies might be steeper, the cumulative operational savings combined with superior efficiency form an overwhelming case for their adoption. Engineers and experts in sustainability emphasize that electric technologies are well-positioned for a greener future, especially as renewable energy increasingly becomes the mainstay of our power grids. Thus, even if gas solutions seem advantageous in the short term, the balance of long-term operational and financial benefits is progressively leaning towards electric options.

## Resource Dependency

In the context of resource dependency, traditional gas technologies and greener alternatives have starkly different implications. Gas-powered equipment, such as ovens or grills in a kitchen, relies on finite fossil fuel resources like fossil gas. This dependency raises concerns about long-term sustainability, given the depletion of these non-renewable resources and the environmental degradation involved in their extraction. Political scientists would also note that this dependence can lead to geopolitical instability, as countries vie for control over fossil fuel reserves.

On the flip side, greener alternatives like solar or wind-powered systems depend on abundant, naturally replenishing resources. Architects and designers appreciate this aspect for its contributions to building sustainability, and chefs value it for the consistent operational costs it can ensure. These technologies harmonize with nature rather than exploit it, aligning with long-term sustainability goals by minimizing habitat destruction and water pollution. By reducing dependency on finite resources, green technologies offer a more sustainable and less risky avenue for the hospitality industry.

## Operational Costs

Navigating operational costs is pivotal for kitchens in the hospitality sector, and choosing between gas and electric technologies, such as induction cooking, can have a substantial effect on financial performance. Gas ranges not only incur expenses from the cost of fossil gas but also necessitate additional outlays for harsh specialized cleaning agents due to stubborn, burnt-on food residues. Conversely, induction cooktops typically require just hot soapy water for cleaning; their lack of open flame or thermal heat sources eliminates the issue of food getting stuck or burnt onto the surface, thereby reducing expenditures on harsh cleaning chemicals and the time needed to clean.

Moreover, the efficiency of induction cooking has real-world financial implications: tests have shown that you can cook nearly twice as much food per hour with induction (70.9 pounds) as compared to gas (38.6 pounds). This increase in throughput directly translates to potential gains in profits, as kitchens can serve more customers in the same time frame. Efficiency also extends to cleanup times. Consider a staff of 20, each making an average of $20 per hour. If induction cooking cuts down cleanup time by 30 minutes per shift, that's a savings of $200 per day (20 staff x $10 for the half-hour saved), $1,400 per week, approximately $6,000 per month, around $18,000 per quarter, and $72,000 annually. These calculations, based on 8-hour shifts and a 40-hour workweek, underline how small operational efficiencies can accumulate into substantial financial savings over time.

## Innovation and Future Potential

In the realm of "Innovation and Future Potential," traditional gas technologies and their greener alternatives are on diverging paths. While gas technologies have seen incremental advancements in efficiency and emissions reductions over the years, their scope for significant environmental improvement is limited. Given their inherent nature as fossil fuel burners, they will continually be associated with greenhouse gas emissions, constraining their future potential for environmental sustainability.

Conversely, greener technologies like induction cooktops and renewable energy systems are in a constant state of evolution. Leveraging advancements in material science, energy storage, and grid integration, these technologies offer considerable room for future enhancements. Their ability to integrate seamlessly with emerging smart grid systems powered by renewable energy sources further accentuates their long-term viability. Engineers, sustainability advocates, and even political scientists see these electric technologies as not just tools for immediate impact but as building blocks for a more sustainable and low-carbon future.

In summary, the comparative analysis of traditional gas technologies and greener electric alternatives in the hospitality sector reveals a compelling narrative. While gas technologies may initially appear efficient and cost-effective, they come with considerable environmental impact, resource dependency, and long-term operational costs that cannot be ignored. On the other hand, electric alternatives such as induction cooking are not only environmentally benign but also offer greater efficiencies, lower operational costs, and exciting opportunities for future innovation. Interdisciplinary insights from fields like engineering, architecture, and culinary further emphasize the long-term sustainability, economic, and operational benefits of transitioning to greener technologies. This comprehensive view challenges the hospitality industry to look beyond short-term gains and consider the broader implications for both the business and the planet.

## 4.2　Cost Benefit Analysis: Evaluating Immediate Costs Against Future Gains and Advantages

The hospitality industry faces a complex landscape when it comes to operational decision-making, especially when dealing with kitchen technologies. Managers must select between various cooking setups, such as traditional gas systems and more modern electric induction systems. This section aims to elucidate how cost-benefit analysis serves as a crucial decision-making tool in these scenarios, enabling a thorough evaluation that goes beyond immediate costs to consider long-term financial and non-financial gains.

**Key Insights**

- Cost-benefit analysis offers a structured methodology for assessing both the tangible and intangible pros and cons of multiple options, making it a universal tool for decision-making.

- Financial metrics such as revenue projections and anticipated cost reductions are fundamental elements in this analytical process.

- Beyond just financial metrics, the methodology is versatile enough to include qualitative factors like customer satisfaction, employee engagement, and environmental impact.

- Advanced applications often include sensitivity and scenario analyses, enabling decision-makers to understand the implications of different variables and conditions.

- The overarching goal is to determine if the long-term value generated by a particular choice outweighs its associated costs, thereby validating it as a sound investment.

## 4.2.1 A Comprehensive Approach to Decision-Making: Unpacking Cost-Benefit Analysis

Cost-benefit analysis isn't just a financial compass. It's a multi-dimensional tool that helps managers assess the full spectrum of factors influencing long-term success, including operational efficiency and broader organizational objectives like sustainability. Managers don't just look at what is financially feasible now; they aim for choices that offer value in the long run and align with organizational goals.

The methodology goes beyond merely listing pros and cons. It provides a structured way to weigh these elements against one another, helping managers navigate the complexities of pivotal operational decisions. This systematic evaluation aids in ensuring that the choice made is both fiscally prudent and sustainably viable, thereby making cost-benefit analysis an indispensable tool in the hospitality sector.

## 4.2.2 Managerial Importance: Why Cost-Benefit Analysis is Foundational

For managers in the hospitality industry, cost-benefit analysis is more than just helpful—it's foundational. This methodological framework enables them to meticulously assess the multifaceted aspects of any significant operational decision. It is particularly helpful in identifying not only the upfront costs but also hidden and long-term expenditures that could have a lasting impact on operational viability.

In addition, the analysis allows managers to evaluate the tangible and intangible benefits that a particular choice could yield. Whether it's immediate cost savings, operational efficiencies, or softer metrics like brand image, a well-executed cost-benefit analysis enables a balanced understanding. This comprehensive view paves the way for decisions that are both empirically grounded and strategically insightful.

### 4.2.3 The Financial Dimensions: More Than Just Initial Investment

When starting a cost-benefit analysis, the immediate focus often goes to the initial capital expenditure. However, this upfront cost is just the tip of the iceberg. A more holistic financial evaluation must consider ongoing operational and maintenance expenses, as well as any hidden costs, such as downtime during transition periods.

For instance, while traditional gas systems may appear cost-effective initially, they often involve additional expenditures like specialized ventilation and frequent maintenance. These costs accumulate over time and can significantly influence the long-term financial viability of the choice. Thus, in-depth financial scrutiny is critical to making well-rounded decisions.

## 4.2.4 The Non-Financial Dimensions: Efficiency, Sustainability, and More

One of the advantages of a comprehensive cost-benefit analysis is its ability to incorporate non-financial factors. These include operational efficiency and ecological sustainability, which are particularly relevant in the debate between gas and electric induction systems. Electric induction systems, for example, are generally more energy-efficient and environmentally friendly than their gas counterparts.

Efficiency gains can translate to shorter cooking times, quicker table turnovers, and higher customer satisfaction—all contributing indirectly to the bottom line. Similarly, as consumers become increasingly eco-conscious, the reputational benefits of sustainable practices can enhance brand value, drawing in more customers and potentially enabling premium pricing.

## 4.2.5 Assessing Risks and Opportunities: Scenario Planning and Opportunity Costs

Any investment involves risk, and a comprehensive cost-benefit analysis must evaluate these uncertainties. This often involves scenario planning and sensitivity analyses that allow for the adjustment of variables to observe their impact. For example, a sudden rise in gas prices or new environmental regulations could significantly affect the cost-benefit ratio.

In every decision-making process, the paths not chosen represent opportunity costs. If you opt for a gas system, you may miss out on the long-term savings and environmental benefits that electric induction technology could offer. Understanding and accounting for these lost opportunities is vital for a complete analysis.

## 4.2.6 Balancing Short-Term and Long-Term Concerns

One of the trickiest aspects of cost-benefit analysis is reconciling immediate, easily quantifiable concerns with longer-term, sometimes more nebulous benefits. Electric induction technologies may require a higher initial outlay but could offer substantial long-term gains in operational savings and sustainability.

Balancing these short-term and long-term factors is critical. Managers must ensure that their choices align with both immediate operational needs and long-term strategic objectives, such as sustainability goals or market competitiveness.

## 4.2.7 Methodological Limitations and Final Observations

While cost-benefit analysis is a powerful tool, it has its limitations. For extensive, long-term projects, certain variables like inflation, interest rates, and the net present value of future cash flows may not be adequately captured. It's essential to recognize these limitations and take them into account in the decision-making process.

Despite these limitations, adopting a comprehensive cost-benefit analysis approach equips organizations to better evaluate risks and rewards. The trend towards electric options in the hospitality sector suggests that when a full spectrum of costs and benefits is considered, more sustainable and operationally efficient choices often come to the fore.

## 4.3 Environmental impact assessment: carbon footprint, pollution, and resource consumption

In the hospitality sector, where choices about kitchen technologies can influence more than just immediate costs and benefits, understanding the broader environmental impact of these decisions becomes vital. This section delves into the foundational aspects of environmental impact, shedding light on the significance of carbon footprints, the consequences of pollution, and the ramifications of resource consumption. By recognizing these elements, businesses can craft informed decisions that align not only with fiscal prudence but also with ecological sustainability.

### 4.3.1 Carbon Footprint: Measuring Our Environmental Footsteps

The term 'carbon footprint' encapsulates the total greenhouse gas emissions, both direct and indirect, attributed to an individual, organization, or specific activity. Represented in carbon dioxide equivalents, it serves as a critical barometer of an entity's environmental impact. A considerable carbon footprint is linked to the exacerbating crisis of climate change, manifesting in rising global temperatures, unpredictable weather patterns, and increasing sea levels. For the hospitality industry, where energy consumption is rife, especially in kitchen operations, the shift towards low-carbon energy sources, enhancement in energy efficiency, and adoption of green practices are imperative steps to diminish the carbon footprint.

## 4.3.2 Pollution: A Multifaceted Threat to Our Ecosystems

When we talk about pollution, we address the release of detrimental substances or contaminants into our environment. These intrusions inflict negative ramifications on ecosystems, human health, and the general quality of our environment. The hospitality industry must be cognizant of:

*Air Pollution: The Invisible Culprit in Kitchen Operations*

In a commercial kitchen, appliances like gas stoves, grills, and ovens release harmful emissions such as nitrogen oxides, carbon monoxide, and particulate matter (like soot and smoke). These substances contribute to air pollution, which can have far-reaching implications:

- **Immediate Health Risks:** Prolonged exposure to these substances can be detrimental to the health of kitchen staff and, in some cases, guests. These risks include respiratory issues and other chronic health problems.
- **Localized Environmental Impact:** Over time, the build-up of these pollutants can degrade air quality, leading to problems like smog, which poses a public health risk.
- **Broader Ecological Consequences:** Air pollutants can travel great distances and contribute to broader environmental issues like acid rain and climate change.

For the hospitality industry, installing high-efficiency exhaust systems and shifting towards eco-friendly kitchen technologies can help mitigate these risks, ensuring a safer, more sustainable operation.

*Water Pollution: The Unseen Consequence of Carelessness*

The hospitality sector generates a substantial amount of waste, including industrial by-products and waste from kitchens. Improper waste management can lead to:

- **Contamination of Local Water Sources:** Chemicals, grease, and other waste materials can seep into the local water supply, posing risks to both humans and aquatic life.
- **Impact on Operational Efficiency:** Contaminated water sources can disrupt a hotel or restaurant's operations, affecting everything from kitchen activities to guest experiences.

Given these ramifications, the importance of responsible waste management and water purification systems cannot be overstated. These steps can safeguard water quality and contribute to broader sustainability goals.

*Pollution from Chemicals and Waste: A Chain Reaction Impacting Food Quality*

Improper disposal of chemicals and waste is not just an issue of cleanliness; it can indirectly affect the quality of the food served in a commercial kitchen.

- **Contaminated Ingredients:** Improper waste disposal can lead to soil pollution, which can then affect the growth conditions for plants and animals. This creates a supply chain risk, as the ingredients sourced for kitchen operations might be compromised.
- **Long-term Sustainability Risks:** The chemical pollution contributes to the degradation of natural ecosystems, which

could eventually affect the availability of high-quality, locally sourced ingredients.

For a sector like hospitality, where the quality of food and sustainability are increasingly intertwined, proper waste management becomes a cornerstone of responsible operations.

By understanding and addressing these types of pollution, the hospitality sector can significantly reduce its environmental impact while ensuring safer, more sustainable operations for staff and guests alike.

## 4.3.3 Resource Consumption: Striking a Balance Between Use and Sustainability

The hospitality sector, with its high demand for resources ranging from energy to ingredients, plays a significant role in the global resource consumption matrix. Excessive utilization of natural assets—be it energy, water, minerals, or raw materials—can lead to rapid resource depletion and consequent ecological harm. Practices such as unchecked water consumption, deforestation for infrastructure, or unregulated mineral extraction pose threats to ecosystems and biodiversity.

For the industry, embracing conservation techniques and sustainable practices is no longer optional. Implementing efficient energy and water usage strategies, endorsing recycling, and committing to responsible sourcing can substantially mitigate the environmental repercussions linked with resource consumption. By integrating these practices, the hospitality industry can ensure a sustainable operational model that respects and supports the environment it thrives in.

With the increasing emphasis on sustainability and environmental responsibility, this section underscores the importance of the hospitality industry understanding and addressing its ecological footprint, especially in kitchen operations. In summary, reducing carbon footprints, minimizing pollution, and adopting sustainable resource consumption practices are crucial for mitigating climate change, protecting ecosystems, and ensuring a healthier environment for future generations.

## Conclusion

Chapter 4 delved into the critical dimensions of evaluating and enhancing the operational efficiency of kitchens in the hospitality sector. It began by exploring the nuts and bolts of energy management, emphasizing the importance of not just choosing energy-efficient appliances but also fostering a culture of energy awareness among staff. From there, we navigated the intricacies of cost-benefit analysis, revealing it as an indispensable tool for making informed decisions. The discussion then expanded to include various financial and non-financial variables, from upfront and recurring costs to intangible benefits and long-term environmental impact.

The latter part of the chapter focused on the overarching theme of sustainability, zeroing in on the environmental consequences of kitchen operations. We unpacked the complexity of pollution—air, water, and chemicals—and its domino effects on both the immediate operational context and broader ecological systems. By the end, the chapter makes a compelling case for an integrated, multi-faceted approach to operational efficiency. It's not merely about cutting costs or choosing the latest technology; it's about aligning every aspect of operations with both immediate needs and long-term sustainability goals. This alignment is crucial for future-proofing businesses in an increasingly competitive and resource-constrained world.

# CHAPTER 5

# ENERGY EFFICIENCY IN HOSPITALITY OPERATIONS

The hospitality industry is an essential part of our global economy, providing comfort and experiences to millions of travelers every day. However, it's also a sector that consumes a substantial amount of energy, which not only impacts operational costs but also has environmental implications. As sustainability becomes an increasingly significant concern, energy efficiency in hospitality operations has gained prominence as a crucial aspect of responsible business practices.

Efficient energy management in the hospitality sector can lead to substantial cost savings, reduce carbon footprints, and enhance overall guest experiences. From optimizing lighting and HVAC systems to adopting eco-friendly practices in laundry and kitchen operations, there are numerous opportunities for hotels, resorts, and restaurants to become more energy-efficient without compromising service quality.

## 5.1 Energy-efficient lighting solutions: LED, motion sensors, and daylight harvesting

The hospitality sector, which has often been scrutinized for its carbon footprint, faces increasing pressure to adopt sustainable practices. Energy efficiency is one pillar of sustainability that offers a dual benefit—reducing both operational costs and environmental impact. At the epicenter of this conversation lies energy-efficient lighting solutions, a subject that transcends disciplines, involving architects in design, engineers in implementation, chefs in kitchen operations, and policymakers in regulation. While the chapter will delve into various aspects of energy efficiency, this section focuses on lighting solutions like LED technology, motion sensors, and daylight harvesting—each of which is crucial for creating an eco-friendly and cost-effective hospitality environment.

**LED Technology**

LED (Light Emitting Diode) technology has revolutionized the lighting industry with its exceptional energy efficiency and durability. It is particularly favored in the hospitality sector, including in hotels, restaurants, and event spaces, for a multitude of reasons. One of the most striking features of LED lights is their significantly lower energy consumption compared to traditional lighting options like incandescent and fluorescent lights—often up to 75% less. This translates into considerable energy savings, which is a boon for any business looking to lower operational costs.

From the perspective of architectural design, LEDs offer unparalleled flexibility due to their compact size and the variety of colors they come in. This allows architects and interior designers to create aesthetically pleasing and functionally efficient lighting solutions.

Chefs and kitchen staff, who require well-lit spaces to ensure food quality and safety, also benefit from the improved lighting quality that LEDs offer.

A less often discussed but highly valuable feature of LED lights is their low heat emission. Traditional lighting solutions not only consume more electricity but also produce more heat, which can be particularly problematic in specific settings within the hospitality industry. Take, for example, a walk-in refrigerator in a hotel or restaurant kitchen. The use of traditional lighting in such a space generates additional heat, forcing the refrigeration system to work harder to maintain a low temperature. This not only consumes more energy but can also compromise the longevity of the refrigeration system.

LED lights, on the other hand, emit far less heat. When used in walk-in refrigerators, this means that the cooling system doesn't have to work as hard to counteract the heat generated by the lighting, leading to more efficient refrigeration. This is a win-win situation—improving energy efficiency, prolonging the lifespan of the refrigeration system, and leading to additional cost savings. Engineers and sustainability experts often point to this particular benefit of LEDs as an example of how thoughtful technology integration can create ripple effects in energy conservation across various systems within a hospitality establishment.

**Motion Sensors**

The integration of motion sensors in lighting systems serves a two-fold purpose: reducing energy waste and enhancing security. Motion sensors ensure that lights are activated only, when necessary, a feature particularly useful in areas of low occupancy such as storerooms, hallways, or bathrooms. Engineers and sustainability experts recommend motion sensors as an easy retrofit to existing lighting systems to achieve immediate energy savings. Moreover, motion-activated lighting systems can add an extra layer of security, a noteworthy benefit for hotels and other lodging establishments.

## Daylight Harvesting

Daylight harvesting goes beyond the realm of mere energy-saving to influence the ambiance and mood of a space. By using sensors and dimming controls, daylight harvesting systems adjust artificial lighting levels based on the amount of natural light available. This serves to not only reduce energy consumption but also create a more pleasant environment. Architects and interior designers often collaborate to optimize the use of natural light in building designs, thereby maximizing the effectiveness of daylight harvesting. For businesses like restaurants and event spaces, the quality of light can significantly impact customer experience, which in turn can have a ripple effect on reviews and, ultimately, revenue.

## Multi-Disciplinary Approach

Energy-efficient lighting solutions embody an interdisciplinary approach, necessitating the expertise of architects for optimum design, engineers for effective implementation, chefs for practical kitchen utility, and policymakers for enforceable regulations. In this context, standards and product specifications like those from ENERGY STAR & EcoChef become particularly important, as they provide a benchmark for energy efficiency that businesses in the hospitality sector can aim for.

By adopting a holistic strategy that incorporates energy-efficient lighting technologies, the hospitality industry can significantly reduce its energy consumption and contribute to a greener, more sustainable future. This goes hand in hand with the broader goals of the green industrial revolution, echoing the overarching themes of this course.

## 5.2 Heating, ventilation, and air conditioning (HVAC) systems: energy-saving techniques and smart controls

Optimizing energy efficiency in hospitality operations is a multifaceted challenge, but one of the most crucial components lies in the heating, ventilation, and air conditioning (HVAC) systems. These systems are often one of the largest energy consumers in a hospitality establishment, from hotels to restaurants. However, with strategic planning and the incorporation of smart controls, it's possible to drastically reduce this energy consumption, leading to not just cost savings but also a lighter carbon footprint.

Energy-efficient HVAC design starts with the selection of the right equipment. High-efficiency boilers, chillers, and heat pumps are essential choices that can result in considerable energy savings. Political science perspectives add that legislative incentives or rebates often support these kinds of sustainable investments, making it economically favorable for businesses to make the switch. From an engineering standpoint, proper insulation and sealing of air leaks are also integral steps, reducing the workload on the HVAC system and thereby consuming less energy. Energy recovery ventilation systems, another innovation, capture waste energy from exhaust airflows to pre-condition incoming fresh air, leading to further energy optimization.

Advancements in smart technology have introduced a variety of intelligent controls that can be integrated into HVAC systems for more refined management. Building Automation Systems (BAS) and programmable thermostats allow for precise control and scheduling of HVAC operations. In spaces with variable occupancy such as conference rooms, lobbies, or dining areas, occupancy sensors and zone-based temperature controls can adjust heating and cooling in real-time. This ensures that climate control is applied only where and when it's necessary, thereby conserving energy. Furthermore, demand-controlled ventilation dynamically adjusts air exchange rates based on actual occupancy, leading to more efficient use of the HVAC system.

These smart controls are not just a boon for energy conservation; they also contribute to guest comfort and well-being, a key concern in the hospitality industry. Chefs and kitchen staff, for instance, benefit from improved air quality and thermal comfort, which can positively impact their productivity and job satisfaction.

To sum up, the hospitality sector can achieve significant reductions in energy consumption and operational costs by adopting energy-saving techniques and smart controls in their HVAC systems. These technologies and practices are aligned with the broader goals of sustainability and offer a concrete pathway for the hospitality industry to contribute positively to the green industrial revolution.

## 5.3 Efficient kitchen equipment and appliances

In the context of the green industrial revolution, the kitchen — often considered the heart of any hospitality operation — plays a significant role in a business's overall carbon footprint. Modern electrified kitchen equipment has come a long way, offering both energy-efficient operation and high performance. Below, we delve into various types of such commercial kitchen appliances and how they can contribute to greener operations.

## Induction Ranges

Induction ranges offer an efficient and precise way of cooking, utilizing electromagnetic fields to heat pans directly, rather than through the inefficient thermal conductivity of a heated element. This results in faster cooking times and more accurate temperature control, allowing chefs to deliver consistent quality. Moreover, induction ranges are considerably safer as they remain cool to the touch, minimizing the risk of burns.

From a sustainability standpoint, induction cooking is incredibly efficient, converting around 90% of the energy it uses into heat. Traditional gas stoves, in contrast, only convert (at best) about 30% to 40% of their energy into usable heat. This reduced energy consumption not only aligns with the goal of lowering carbon footprints but also results in cost savings over time.

## Demand Control Kitchen Ventilation and Heat Recovery Hoods

Demand Control Kitchen Ventilation (DCKV) systems are designed to adjust the speed of exhaust and make-up fans in the ventilation hood based on real-time kitchen conditions. Traditional systems often run at full speed, wasting energy during slower periods. DCKV systems use sensors to determine cooking load and adjust fan speeds accordingly, significantly saving on energy costs.

Heat recovery hoods take the sustainability element a step further. These systems capture the waste heat from cooking appliances and use it to pre-heat water or even the incoming fresh air, further reducing the energy load on heating systems. This can be particularly useful for large-scale operations where both hot water and heating demands are high.

## Heat Recovery Dishwashers

Commercial dishwashers are typically high-energy appliances. Heat recovery dishwashers capture the steam generated during the washing cycle and use it to heat incoming cold water. This drastically reduces the energy needed to heat water and provides significant cost savings.

Engineers point out the efficiency of such a closed-loop system, noting that it also eliminates the need for additional venting to expel steam, further conserving energy. For businesses, this means lower operational costs and a smaller carbon footprint, making heat recovery dishwashers a wise investment for any kitchen focused on sustainability.

## Combination Ovens

Combination ovens, which offer convection, steaming, and combination cooking in a single appliance, provide multiple cooking options and are incredibly energy efficient. They enable precise temperature and humidity control, allowing for a wide range of cooking techniques without the need to transfer food between different appliances.

Combination ovens are particularly favored by chefs for their versatility and efficiency. They not only save on energy but, by replacing a steamer and an oven, also on kitchen space, another valuable resource in commercial operations. Their adaptability and multi-functionality mean fewer appliances are needed, thereby reducing both initial investment and ongoing energy costs.

## Refrigeration Using High-Efficiency Refrigerants (e.g., R290)

Commercial kitchens have long grappled with the energy-intensive nature of refrigeration. Yet, the advent of refrigerators using high-efficiency refrigerants like R290 has opened the door to considerably more energy-efficient and environmentally friendly options. Unlike its traditional counterparts such as R404a, which has a staggering Global Warming Potential (GWP) of 3,920, R290 has a markedly lower GWP of just 3.

This shift to refrigerants like R290 is more than just an environmental boon; it's also an operational advantage. These high-efficiency refrigerants enable the refrigerator's compressor to cycle on and off less frequently, resulting in more efficient operation and energy conservation. Governments around the world are beginning to recognize these benefits, offering incentives to organizations that make the switch. As such, opting for refrigerators that utilize R290 or similar refrigerants is not only an environmentally responsible decision but also an economically savvy one.

## AI-Driven Equipment

Artificial Intelligence (AI) is making its way into commercial kitchens, enabling smart ovens, fryers, and even inventory systems that learn from usage patterns to optimize performance. These systems can adjust cooking times and temperatures, suggest maintenance schedules, and even automate inventory tracking, leading to more efficient operations.

The potential for AI in reducing food waste is also substantial, an issue particularly important for sustainability. AI-driven equipment can analyze patterns in food usage, helping chefs and managers make more informed decisions about inventory, reducing waste, and thereby conserving both financial and environmental resources.

In summary, the advent of energy-efficient, smart kitchen equipment offers hospitality businesses a practical route to significantly reduce their energy consumption and environmental impact. Investing in such technologies will not only result in immediate operational savings but also align businesses with the broader societal shift towards sustainability and responsible resource usage.

## 5.4 Integrating Automation and Smart Technology for Energy Optimization in the Hospitality Industry

The integration of automation and smart technology is rapidly becoming an essential aspect of energy management across various industries, including the hospitality sector. Utilizing sophisticated building management systems (BMS) along with Internet of Things (IoT) devices, hotels, restaurants, and other hospitality businesses can actively monitor and manage energy consumption in real-time. This real-time management leads to enhanced energy efficiency, operational cost savings, and a reduction in the environmental impact.

Automated systems, through the use of smart sensors and meters, can precisely adjust lighting, HVAC settings, and even kitchen equipment operations according to various parameters such as occupancy levels, time of day, and specific energy needs. Such automation not only optimizes energy consumption but also offers insights into energy usage patterns. This data-driven approach allows businesses to identify areas where improvements can be made and then deploy targeted energy-saving strategies, such as the implementation of high-efficiency refrigerants or heat recovery systems.

In addition, automation enables the hospitality sector to participate in demand-response programs effectively. During periods of peak energy demand, automated systems can make temporary adjustments to energy consumption patterns, thereby reducing strain on the grid and contributing to overall energy conservation efforts. The seamless integration of renewable energy sources like solar panels with these automated systems can further amplify energy efficiency gains and diminish dependency on traditional energy grids.

The use of automation and smart technology transcends the boundaries of mere cost-saving and reaches into the realm of sustainability and responsible business practices. By adopting these technologies, the hospitality industry is better equipped to meet the dual objectives of operational efficiency and environmental stewardship, key components in the broader context of the emerging green industrial revolution.

## 5.5 Influence of ENERGY STAR© Product Certification & Benchmarking

In today's rapidly evolving world, the concept of sustainability plays a critical role in the longevity and reputation of any industry, particularly in hospitality. With increasing awareness of climate change and its far-reaching implications, both consumers and stakeholders are demanding more responsible practices from businesses. It's in this high-stakes environment that the ENERGY STAR program shines as a beacon guiding the hospitality sector toward greener operations. Established in 1992, the program has set stringent criteria for energy-efficient products, commercial buildings

& industrial plants, influencing a sea of change in the way the hospitality industry approaches energy consumption, cost management, and environmental stewardship. This section aims to provide a comprehensive examination of ENERGY STAR's role, its transformative impact from its inception to its current-day ramifications, and its broader influence, including on design and chemical standards in the hospitality industry.

## What is ENERGY STAR?

ENERGY STAR is a market-transformation program established by the United States Environmental Protection Agency (EPA) and the Department of Energy (DOE) with the primary objective of promoting energy efficiency across various sectors. The voluntary public-private partnership program provides guidelines and certification for over 75 products, ranging from appliances and electronics to building materials and commercial food service equipment. The hallmark of ENERGY STAR-certified products is their high energy efficiency, guaranteed to save energy and reduce greenhouse gas emissions without compromising performance. ENERGY STAR's blue logo serves as a recognizable mark of quality and sustainability, helping consumers and businesses make informed decisions about their purchases.

Within the hospitality industry, the ENERGY STAR certification has been particularly transformative. For a sector that has a multitude of energy needs, including heating, lighting, cooling, and operating a variety of kitchen appliances, ENERGY STAR provides a roadmap for sustainable operations. Certified products must meet stringent energy-efficient criteria set by the EPA, thus offering the hospitality industry an objective and credible way to implement and promote energy-saving measures. By adopting ENERGY STAR-certified appliances and equipment, hospitality businesses can significantly reduce their operating costs while lessening their environmental impact. This adoption has not only influenced product design but also has set new industry standards for energy consumption, forming a cornerstone of modern sustainability initiatives in hospitality.

## How Did the Industry Look Before ENERGY STAR?

Prior to the introduction of the ENERGY STAR program, the hospitality industry was navigating a landscape with limited focus on energy efficiency and sustainability. Hotels, restaurants, and other hospitality ventures operated primarily on criteria such as performance, cost, and customer satisfaction, with little attention given to the environmental impact of their choices. Appliances and equipment were often selected based on their upfront costs rather than their lifetime energy use, leading to a noticeable lack of energy-efficient options. This absence of standardized energy-efficient practices made it challenging for businesses to evaluate the long-term cost and environmental implications of their operational decisions.

Moreover, the absence of a product energy efficiency criteria like ENERGY STAR meant that claims regarding energy efficiency were largely not standardized, potentially leading to misleading or exaggerated assertions from manufacturers. Businesses that wanted to invest in energy-efficient technologies had to wade through a morass of conflicting information and inconsistent product labeling. This made it difficult to make well-informed decisions, both in terms of reducing operational costs and lowering carbon footprint. As a result, the industry was characterized by higher energy costs, greater $CO_2$ emissions, and a missed opportunity for aligning business objectives with environmental stewardship. ENERGY STAR emerged as a response to this gap, offering a trusted benchmark that has since reshaped the industry's approach to sustainability and energy management.

## What Did the Development of ENERGY STAR Look Like?

The ENERGY STAR program was introduced in 1992 by the United States Environmental Protection Agency (EPA) as a voluntary labeling program designed to identify and promote energy-efficient products to reduce greenhouse gas emissions. Initially, the program only covered computer and printer products but quickly expanded to other categories, including home appliances and eventually to the commercial sector which envelops the hospitality industry. The development phase involved rigorous testing protocols and criteria for what would constitute an "energy-efficient" product. The objective was not just to reduce energy consumption but also to ensure that energy savings did not come at the expense of product performance or user experience.

In its development stage, ENERGY STAR worked closely with manufacturers, testing organizations, and other stakeholders to develop criteria that were both ambitious and achievable. Setting the standards too low would render the certification meaningless, while setting them too high might discourage participation. It was essential to strike a balance. Moreover, the program was designed to be dynamic, adapting and updating its criteria to keep pace with technological innovations. This iterative approach ensured that the ENERGY STAR label would remain a symbol of genuine energy efficiency, encouraging ongoing improvements and investments in sustainable technologies. Over the years, the ENERGY STAR program has undergone several updates and expansions, continually adapting to cover new sectors and technologies, including the vast array of equipment and operational needs present in the hospitality industry.

## How Did the Industry Look After ENERGY STAR Came Out?

The introduction of ENERGY STAR brought a transformative shift to the hospitality sector, most notably by providing a trusted standard for assessing the energy efficiency of appliances, equipment, and even entire buildings. Prior to ENERGY STAR, businesses had to rely on a variety of metrics and claims from manufacturers, which could be confusing and sometimes misleading. With the advent of ENERGY STAR, the industry now had a unified, authoritative benchmark against which to measure energy performance. This resulted in a wave of upgrades and changes across the industry as manufacturers sought to certify their products to ENERGY STAR and to showcase their commitment to sustainability.

Beyond individual appliances and products, the ENERGY STAR program extended its reach to cover entire building operations, including heating, ventilation, and air conditioning (HVAC) systems, lighting solutions, and even architectural design. Hotels and other facilities in the hospitality sector could now achieve ENERGY STAR certification by benchmarking facility performance with a score of 75 or higher in the free Portfolio Manager tool for whole-building operations, indicating to consumers and stakeholders that they operated at the highest standard of energy efficiency. While restaurants cannot currently achieve ENERGY STAR certification, benchmarking provides a baseline Energy utilization Intensity (EUI) number – compared to other U.S. restaurants from which to track improvements. This has not only led to a more competitive marketplace for energy-efficient solutions but also contributed to the broader goals of carbon footprint reduction. According to EPA estimates, the ENERGY STAR program helped businesses save approximately $35 billion in energy costs and prevented 350 million metric tons of greenhouse gas emissions in a single year. These changes reflect a radical departure from the days before ENERGY STAR, moving the industry significantly closer to sustainability and environmentally responsible operation.

## Carbon Footprint Pre and Post ENERGY STAR

Before the advent of ENERGY STAR, the hospitality industry faced a significant challenge in terms of its carbon footprint. Many businesses operated under an archaic model of energy usage that heavily relied on fossil fuels and inefficient appliances, contributing to considerable greenhouse gas emissions. There were few incentives or standardized methods for businesses to understand the environmental impact of their operations, leading to a landscape that was, by and large, unsustainable. According to various estimates, the hospitality industry, including hotels and restaurants, was responsible for a significant proportion of commercial energy consumption, often without any clear pathways to reduce their carbon emissions meaningfully.

The post-ENERGY STAR landscape, however, paints a more optimistic picture. The program provides a straightforward way to identify and promote energy-efficient practices and products, allowing businesses to make informed decisions that directly affect their carbon footprint. This was not limited to just energy-efficient lighting or HVAC systems but extended to how food is stored in commercial refrigerators, how rooms are heated, and even how dishwashers are run in commercial kitchens. As businesses began to adopt ENERGY STAR-certified products, the collective carbon footprint saw substantial reductions. According to the U.S. Environmental Protection Agency (EPA), the ENERGY STAR program has been instrumental in reducing billions of pounds of greenhouse gas emissions since its inception. Hospitality businesses that have fully adopted ENERGY STAR-certified products and practices often report significant drops in their carbon footprint, aligning not only with global sustainability efforts but also resonating well with an increasingly eco-conscious consumer base.

## Importance of ENERGY STAR

ENERGY STAR serves as more than just a seal of approval for energy-efficient products; it has become a vital tool for businesses in the hospitality industry to evaluate and implement sustainable practices. By providing a clear and attainable framework for energy conservation, it allows businesses to not only reduce their operating costs but also demonstrate a commitment to environmental stewardship. As sustainability becomes increasingly important to consumers, being able to brandish the ENERGY STAR label offers a competitive edge in the market. The program sets criteria that go beyond mere compliance; it motivates businesses to strive for continual improvement, thereby further reducing their carbon footprint over time. The specifications for ENERGY STAR certification are reviewed and updated regularly, ensuring that the program evolves along with technological advancements, thereby maintaining its relevance and utility.

Moreover, the ENERGY STAR program has been a catalyst for the development and adoption of other sustainability certifications and standards in the industry. Building on ENERGY STAR's foundation, certifications like LEED (Leadership in Energy and Environmental Design), WELL (Well Building Standard), ILFI (International Living Future Institute), EcoChef, and BREEAM (Building Research Establishment Environmental Assessment Method) have emerged to address various aspects of sustainability, from building design and construction to employee well-being and food preparation techniques. These certifications often complement the ENERGY STAR specifications, providing businesses in the hospitality sector with a comprehensive roadmap to sustainability. The success of ENERGY STAR has shown that environmental sustainability and profitability can indeed go hand-in-hand, inspiring a whole new generation of green certifications and standards.

## ENERGY STAR Specifications

ENERGY STAR product specifications include energy efficiency, energy consumption, and water consumption criteria that products must meet to earn the program's certification. The specifications are formulated through a rigorous data-driven process and are reviewed periodically to ensure they remain up-to-date with technological advancements. For the hospitality industry, these specifications are particularly impactful as they cover a wide range of equipment and appliances commonly found in hotels and restaurants, such as commercial refrigerators, dishwashers, and HVAC systems. Each product category has specific energy performance indicators that must be met or exceeded. For instance, ENERGY STAR-certified commercial dishwashers must use less energy and water per cycle compared to non-certified models. The specifications provide a roadmap for manufacturers to develop more energy-efficient products, and for business owners to make informed purchasing decisions.

The specifications extend beyond just appliances and equipment. ENERGY STAR also has a certification program for commercial buildings, which is highly relevant for hotels, conference centers, and other large facilities in the hospitality industry. To qualify, a building must earn an ENERGY STAR score of 75 or higher, indicating that it performs better than at least 75% of similar buildings nationwide in terms of energy efficiency. This is calculated using the EPA's online energy management tool, Portfolio Manager, which measures a building's energy performance. By following these guidelines, businesses can significantly reduce their energy consumption, lower their operating costs, and decrease their environmental footprint, all while providing the same or better level of service to their customers.

**Effects Beyond Equipment**

ENERGY STAR's success in revolutionizing energy efficiency standards and practices has had a ripple effect, inspiring the EPA to create several impactful programs aimed at enhancing sustainability across various sectors, including hospitality.

*WaterSense*: Launched in 2006, WaterSense was developed by the EPA with a similar ethos to ENERGY STAR but focused on water conservation. It sets stringent criteria for water-efficient products and promotes water-saving practices. In the hospitality industry, this program has encouraged the adoption of low-flow fixtures, faucets, and efficient irrigation systems, significantly reducing water usage in hotels and restaurants while maintaining quality service.

*Safer Choice*: This program, established in 1997 but expanded later, concentrates on the development and promotion of safer chemical products. Within the hospitality sector, it has encouraged the use of environmentally friendly cleaning products and chemicals, ensuring guest and staff safety while minimizing environmental impact. Hotels and resorts have increasingly shifted towards safer cleaning solutions, aligning with this program's guidelines.

*Sustainable Purchasing*: Inspired by ENERGY STAR's success in setting benchmarks, the EPA initiated programs to encourage sustainable procurement practices. By providing guidelines for purchasing environmentally preferable products, this initiative has influenced the hospitality industry to source goods and services that meet specific environmental and social criteria. This includes sourcing locally produced food, furniture made from sustainable materials, and energy-efficient appliances.

*Sustainable Management of Food*: Recognizing the significant impact of food waste on the environment, this program emerged to address the issue within the hospitality sector. It promotes strategies to reduce, recover, and recycle food waste, encouraging hotels and restaurants to implement composting, food donation programs, and efficient kitchen practices. By doing so, they minimize their ecological footprint and contribute to a more sustainable food system.

Each of these programs reflects a response to the success of ENERGY STAR, employing similar strategies to set standards, provide specifications, and incentivize industries like hospitality to embrace sustainable practices. They collectively contribute to a more environmentally conscious and responsible approach to business operations.

## Importance in Building Certifications

ENERGY STAR's reach extends into the realm of building certifications, acting as a foundation upon which other sustainability certifications are built. It has become a prerequisite or a significant contributor to various global building certifications like LEED (Leadership in Energy and Environmental Design), WELL, ILFI (International Living Future Institute), EcoChef, and BREEAM (Building Research Establishment Environmental Assessment Method). These certifications often require that a building meet certain energy efficiency standards, for which having ENERGY STAR-certified appliances and systems can earn significant points or even be a prerequisite.

In the hospitality industry, this is particularly noteworthy. Hotels, resorts, and restaurants are increasingly seeking these certifications to appeal to an eco-conscious consumer base and to comply with tightening environmental regulations. Not only do these certifications offer a competitive edge, but they also typically lead to operational cost savings in the long run. For example, a LEED-certified building often incorporates ENERGY STAR-certified HVAC systems, lighting, and kitchen appliances as part of its broader sustainability strategy. Such credentials can elevate a brand's image and attract a clientele that values sustainability, thereby impacting not just the environment but also the bottom line. ENERGY STAR serves as a trusted symbol for energy efficiency, providing a ripple effect that amplifies its impact far beyond individual appliances to the structure as a whole.

## 5.6 LEED Certification & Its Importance in the Hospitality Industry

As climate change and environmental concerns continue to gain public attention, the onus is increasingly falling on industries, including hospitality, to adopt sustainable practices. Amidst this backdrop, LEED (Leadership in Energy and Environmental Design) certification has emerged as a critical benchmark for environmental responsibility and sustainable operation. Developed and administered by the U.S. Green Building Council (USGBC), LEED sets rigorous standards for everything from energy efficiency to water conservation and waste reduction. Within the specialized realm of the hospitality sector, where energy consumption and waste can be particularly high due to the needs of hotels, restaurants, and event spaces, achieving LEED certification signifies a meaningful commitment to mitigating environmental impact.

Understanding LEED and its implications is not just beneficial but essential for anyone in the hospitality industry—from architects and designers laying out energy-efficient kitchen spaces to political science experts influencing sustainability regulations, and chefs opting for more efficient cooking methods. This section aims to provide an in-depth look at what LEED certification entails, why it is crucial in the hospitality industry, and how it interacts with other industry standards. We'll examine the criteria that need to be met for LEED certification, its increasing importance as a hallmark of sustainable operation, and how it complements other certifications like ENERGY STAR, WELL, and EcoChef. By doing so, we aim to create a comprehensive understanding that empowers professionals to make informed decisions in their pursuit of sustainable practices within the hospitality sector.

## What is LEED?

Created in 1998 LEED, or Leadership in Energy and Environmental Design, is a globally recognized certification system that evaluates the environmental performance and sustainability of buildings and communities. Originated in the United States and administered by the U.S. Green Building Council (USGBC), LEED provides a comprehensive framework for assessing a broad spectrum of elements that impact a building's environmental footprint, including site selection, energy and water usage, materials and resources, and indoor air quality. The system awards different levels of certification based on a point system that grades the performance of buildings or projects against these varied criteria. The levels range from Certified to Silver, Gold, and Platinum, each representing a higher degree of commitment to sustainable practices.

For the hospitality industry, LEED certification is often sought for new buildings and extensive renovations, and it can apply to everything from individual hotels to entire hotel chains, restaurants, event spaces, and even cruise ships. LEED has also extended its purview to include "LEED for Cities and Communities," focusing on creating sustainable, livable urban environments, which has implications for the larger hospitality ecosystems like tourist districts and resort communities. The LEED certification process involves stringent third-party verification, ensuring that the practices and features are not just claimed but also demonstrably effective in reducing environmental impact. Achieving LEED certification is an intricate process requiring the expertise of architects, engineers, sustainability consultants, and sometimes even political science experts who understand the regulations and incentives at play. By opting for LEED certification, a hospitality business not only signals its commitment to sustainability but often also reaps financial benefits through energy savings and tax incentives, making it a win-win situation for both the planet and the profit margin.

## Criteria for LEED Certification

The criteria for LEED certification are broken down into several major categories that cover a broad range of sustainability considerations. These include Sustainable Sites, Water Efficiency, Energy and Atmosphere, Materials and Resources, Indoor Environmental Quality, and Innovation in Design. Each category consists of specific prerequisites and credits that a project can earn to accumulate points toward certification. Prerequisites are the essential elements that every LEED project must meet, while credits offer flexibility, allowing the project to earn points in ways that are most applicable and practical to them.

In the context of the hospitality industry, these criteria can apply in a multitude of ways. For instance, Sustainable Sites can relate to the location of the hotel or restaurant and its access to public transportation, or the use of landscaping that requires minimal water. Water Efficiency might evaluate not only the building's plumbing and waste systems but also how a hotel swimming pool or spa manages water usage. Energy and Atmosphere will examine energy source quality, efficiency of HVAC systems, and the integration of renewable energy sources, among other aspects. Materials and Resources assess the sustainability of building materials and waste management, crucial in industries like hospitality where renovation cycles can be frequent. Indoor Environmental Quality looks at elements like air filtration systems, which can be particularly significant in settings like hotels where many people are staying in an enclosed space. Lastly, Innovation in

Design allows for extra points for innovative solutions that meet the objectives of LEED but aren't explicitly mentioned in the criteria.

Navigating the LEED criteria requires a multidisciplinary approach, often involving architects, engineers, interior designers, and sustainability experts to ensure that all aspects of a project are aligned with LEED requirements. This often means that the planning stage for a new hotel or renovation project can be more complex and time-consuming, but the long-term benefits of energy savings, improved guest experience, and a stronger brand image make it a worthwhile investment.

## Importance of LEED in the Hospitality Industry

The hospitality industry is increasingly under pressure to operate sustainably, not just for ethical or environmental reasons, but also due to growing consumer awareness and demand for eco-friendly practices. In this context, LEED certification serves as a rigorous and internationally recognized benchmark that provides guests with assurance that a hospitality business is genuinely committed to sustainability. LEED certification can significantly differentiate a hotel, restaurant, or conference center in a crowded and competitive marketplace. Moreover, it can attract a more discerning clientele who are willing to pay a premium for accommodations that align with their own sustainability values.

In addition to customer attraction, LEED certification offers a variety of operational advantages. These include energy and water savings that translate into reduced operational costs over the long term. The certification also promotes healthier indoor spaces, thereby potentially improving guest satisfaction and, consequently, ratings and reviews. This multi-faceted value proposition—encompassing both ethical and economic considerations—is driving an increasing number of hospitality businesses to seek LEED certification. As more stakeholders like investors and shareholders take interest in the sustainability efforts of companies, being LEED-certified also contributes to a stronger market position. For many in the industry, LEED has become less of an option and more of a necessity for future-proofing their operations.

Another overlooked yet crucial aspect is employee morale and retention. Studies have shown that working in LEED-certified buildings can improve employee satisfaction and productivity. This is especially critical in the hospitality sector, known for its high turnover rates. When employees know they are contributing to a greater good, it creates a positive working environment, and this positivity often extends to their interactions with guests. From reducing the carbon footprint to realizing cost savings, and from attracting a targeted customer base to retaining satisfied employees, the importance of LEED certification in the hospitality industry is comprehensive and continually expanding.

## LEED and Its Relation to Other Certifications

While LEED is a globally recognized green building certification system, it's important to note that it's not the only player in the field of sustainability certifications. LEED often serves as a stepping stone or complement to other environmental and sustainability certification programs, each with its unique focus and set of criteria. For instance, WELL Building Standards concentrate primarily on human health and well-being within the built environment, integrating architectural and operational measures that aim to boost occupant well-being. The integration of LEED and WELL can therefore provide a holistic approach to both environmental sustainability and human health within the same framework, a combination that is especially valuable in the hospitality industry where customer experience is paramount.

Similarly, certifications like BREEAM (Building Research Establishment Environmental Assessment Method) in the UK and EcoChef focus on different but overlapping aspects of sustainable building and operations. The former is one of the oldest and most widely used methods for assessing, rating, and certifying the sustainability of buildings, while the latter is the youngest and focuses specifically on sustainable practices in commercial kitchens. Other certifications such as ILFI (International Living Future Institute) offer even more stringent sustainability goals, like net-zero energy consumption. Then there is the ENERGY STAR program, which could be seen as a complementary certification focusing on energy-efficient appliances and building systems. All of these certifications can co-exist, providing multiple layers of verification for a building's or business's sustainability efforts.

In the broader hospitality industry, having multiple certifications can offer a robust portrayal of a commitment to sustainability, attracting a wide range of consumers interested in different facets of eco-friendliness and health. On the flip side, it can also benefit the businesses themselves by helping them qualify for various types of incentives, grants, or loans aimed at promoting sustainable practices. Therefore, understanding the landscape of available certifications, including LEED, can enable hospitality businesses to make informed decisions that align with their sustainability goals, operational needs, and market positioning.

## The Future: Beyond LEED

As the standards for sustainability evolve, so too does LEED. Continuous revisions and updates to the LEED criteria keep it at the forefront of sustainable building practices. In the hospitality industry, we can expect to see a growing number of LEED-certified properties, each striving for higher levels of certification as new technologies and methods become available. The trajectory indicates a future where LEED or similar certifications could very well become the standard rather than the exception, driving the entire industry towards a more sustainable, eco-conscious future.

## 5.7 EcoChef Certification: Pioneering a Decarbonized Future in the Hospitality Industry

In an era where the urgency of sustainable practices cannot be overstated, the hospitality industry has been grappling with a growing responsibility to mitigate its impact on the environment and improve working conditions for its staff. While many traditional practices in commercial kitchens contribute to large carbon footprints and other environmental concerns, the industry has been slow to innovate and adopt more sustainable models. This is where the newest certification on the market, EcoChef, enters the scene. Developed by Forward Dining Solutions, EcoChef is the world's first electric kitchen rating system that aims to standardize the conception, construction, and operation of commercial kitchens. Its goal is nothing short of transformative: to decarbonize the hospitality industry, improve the well-being of its workforce, and set new benchmarks for sustainable excellence. In the following sections, we delve into the numerous ways EcoChef addresses the complex challenges facing the hospitality industry, heralding a more sustainable and equitable future for all its stakeholders.

By systematically addressing the most pressing issues—ranging from energy efficiency to employee well-being—EcoChef offers a comprehensive blueprint for the industry. Its guidelines are designed to be both achievable and ambitious, making it a critical tool for any hospitality business committed to responsible operation. The EcoChef certification program is more than just a set of guidelines; it's a movement aimed at raising the bar for what is possible within sustainable culinary practices. In doing so, it not only promises to improve the livelihoods of those in the industry but also sets a high standard for environmental responsibility that has the potential to inspire the sector at large.

## The Need for Change: Confronting Long-Standing Issues in the Hospitality Industry

The hospitality industry is no stranger to challenges that require urgent attention. From kitchens equipped with outdated, energy-guzzling appliances to poorly ventilated workspaces, many establishments are stuck in a paradigm that fails to prioritize both environmental sustainability and employee well-being. This is not just a question of modernization; it's a multifaceted issue that has direct implications for the health of the planet and the people who make the industry run.

The current status quo contributes to an alarmingly high carbon footprint for the hospitality sector. Conventional energy sources, often derived from fossil fuels, not only elevate operational costs but also exacerbate climate change. Moreover, lackluster working conditions, from insufficient ventilation to inadequate safety measures, put employee health at risk and can lead to high turnover rates and reduced productivity. These issues are not isolated; they are interrelated symptoms of an industry in need of holistic solutions. The existing conditions have put the industry on an unsustainable path that amplifies environmental degradation while compromising the well-being of its workforce. Changing these conditions is not just a matter of ethical or regulatory compliance; it's a pressing necessity for the industry to evolve and thrive in a rapidly changing world.

EcoChef certification enters this challenging landscape with a robust solution aimed at transforming commercial kitchen spaces. By doing so, it hopes to address these systemic issues, making it imperative for the hospitality sector to take note and act. Adopting EcoChef's comprehensive guidelines could be the much-needed step towards forging a sustainable and humane path for the industry, tackling both its environmental footprint and the quality of life for its employees.

## Advantages of Certification: A New Horizon for Sustainable Hospitality

The EcoChef certification is not merely a badge of honor; it is a comprehensive framework that offers a multitude of benefits to the hospitality industry. Achieving this certification signals a commitment to adopting energy-efficient practices and cutting-edge technologies that substantially mitigate environmental impact. It's a statement that tells both the consumer and the broader industry that a certified establishment is serious about its responsibilities toward sustainability.

Beyond the environmental benefits, the certification brings a unique market advantage. As consumers become increasingly conscious of their ecological impact, they are more likely to choose services that align with their values. EcoChef certification allows businesses to distinguish themselves as pioneers in sustainability, thereby attracting a more dedicated and eco-conscious customer base. This not only enhances an establishment's reputation but can also translate to higher profitability as consumers are often willing to pay a premium to support establishments who have a commitment to sustainability.

Moreover, the certification fosters a more fulfilling and healthful working environment for employees. By adhering to EcoChef's standards, establishments can enhance the comfort, safety, and well-being of their staff, which can result in greater job satisfaction and productivity. When employees feel good about where they work, they are more likely to stay, reducing turnover and the associated costs of training new staff. In this way, the EcoChef certification sets a new bar for excellence, creating a ripple effect that benefits not just the establishment itself but also the industry as a whole.

Overall, EcoChef certification serves as a catalyst for comprehensive change, offering hospitality businesses a pathway to operate more sustainably and responsibly. Through streamlined operations, cost savings, and market differentiation, EcoChef certification not only paves the way for a greener future but also gives forward-thinking establishments a competitive edge in an increasingly crowded marketplace.

**EcoChef Standards: Redefining Excellence in Commercial Kitchens**

EcoChef standards are meticulously designed to address the critical aspects that define a sustainable commercial kitchen. The program is grounded in six essential pillars—Energy Efficiency, Comfort,

Indoor Air Quality, Performance, Waste, and Innovation—that collectively create a harmonized environment where culinary excellence meets ecological responsibility.

- **Energy Efficiency: Pioneering Sustainability through Efficiency**

Energy Efficiency is the cornerstone of the EcoChef program. By integrating cutting-edge technologies and industry best practices, the standard aims to drastically reduce energy consumption within commercial kitchens. This is vital not only for economic reasons but also for the planet. Reduced energy consumption translates into a lower carbon footprint, aligning with broader efforts to mitigate climate change. By taking significant steps toward energy-efficient practices, commercial kitchens set the stage for an ecologically sustainable culinary landscape.

- **Comfort: Nurturing Well-being with Optimal Design**

The Comfort pillar emphasizes creating a workspace that enhances the well-being of kitchen staff. Ergonomic design, temperature-controlled settings, and thoughtful layout are just some of the aspects considered to improve both the physical and emotional health of employees. A comfortable and well-designed workspace can lead to increased productivity and job satisfaction, enriching the overall work environment.

- **Indoor Air Quality: Breathing Life into Culinary Spaces**

Indoor Air Quality (IAQ) is another crucial pillar, aimed at promoting a healthier atmosphere within commercial kitchens. Proper ventilation, air filtration, and pollution control are key components. High-quality IAQ benefits not only the kitchen staff but also enhances the overall ambiance of the dining area, reinforcing the establishment's commitment to environmental stewardship and customer experience.

- **Performance: Elevating Culinary Mastery & Efficiency**

Performance is a pillar that focuses on the operational effectiveness of the kitchen, from cooking techniques to the efficient utilization of resources. It underscores the imperative of achieving culinary excellence without compromising on sustainability objectives. Improved performance often results from adopting high performance energy-efficient equipment, thereby forging a synergy between economic and environmental benefits.

- **Waste: Curbing Excess, Championing Resourcefulness**

Waste management is a critical concern in commercial kitchens. The Waste pillar aims to revolutionize how kitchens manage their waste by promoting reduction, recycling, and responsible disposal. It challenges establishments to re-examine their waste generation and disposal practices, fostering a culture of resourcefulness that aligns with both economic sensibility and ecological responsibility.

- **Innovation: Envisioning a Future Beyond Standards**

Lastly, Innovation is the pillar that propels the culinary sector into uncharted territories. This component encourages establishments to go beyond existing norms and protocols to set new sustainability benchmarks. Whether it's pioneering a zero-waste cooking method, integrating renewable energy sources, or having staff that is EcoChef certified, Innovation aims to push the envelope on what's possible within the realms of environmental stewardship and culinary artistry.

Together, these pillars form a comprehensive framework that positions EcoChef as a transformative force, steering the hospitality sector towards a more sustainable and responsible future.

## Forging a Sustainable Culinary Era: The Broader Implications of EcoChef

This certification program goes beyond being a mere emblem of quality; it represents the crucial paradigm shifts needed in the hospitality industry to confront climate change, environmental degradation, and resource depletion, all while maintaining an unwavering focus on quality, performance, and efficient throughput. EcoChef is laying down the tracks for the future, setting forth a multi-faceted framework that goes beyond food preparation to touch every aspect of commercial kitchen operations—from energy consumption and waste management to employee well-being and innovation. By integrating these elements into a cohesive set of guidelines and practices, EcoChef is driving a fundamental change in how the hospitality industry views its role in sustainable development.

The transformative power of EcoChef doesn't stop at commercial kitchens. It has a ripple effect, influencing suppliers, consumers, and policymakers to rethink how the hospitality sector operates. By fostering a culture of sustainable practices and highlighting the business advantages of going green, the program transcends traditional boundaries to effect change at multiple levels. Achieving EcoChef certification is not merely a technical accomplishment; it's an ethical commitment to a new era of responsible, resource-efficient, and innovative hospitality.

## Enhanced Reputation

In a world where consumers are increasingly focused on sustainability and environmental responsibility, obtaining an EcoChef certification can boost a business's reputation. The certification serves as a transparent indicator that the establishment is committed to reducing its carbon footprint, enhancing energy efficiency, and promoting sustainable practices. This not only garners trust from customers but also sets the business apart in a competitive market, where being "green" is becoming a key differentiator. An enhanced reputation can have far-reaching implications, such as attracting investors who prioritize sustainability, and securing partnerships with like-minded organizations.

## Market Advantage

EcoChef certification does more than improve a business's image; it also offers a tangible market advantage. As sustainability becomes a pressing concern for consumers, establishments with an EcoChef certification are likely to attract a growing segment of eco-conscious patrons. These customers are often willing to pay a premium for services they consider environmentally responsible, providing an opportunity for increased revenue. Additionally, having a certification like EcoChef can provide a competitive edge when bidding for contracts or entering new markets where environmental standards are a key consideration. This market advantage is increasingly important as municipalities, states, and countries adopt stricter environmental regulations, effectively future proofing the business.

## Cost Savings and Environmental Priorities

Another significant advantage lies in operational cost savings. The EcoChef standards focus on efficient energy use, waste management, and optimized performance—all of which contribute to lower operating costs in the long run. But the benefits extend beyond economics. Reduced carbon footprint, waste reduction, and conservation of natural resources are crucial environmental gains that come from implementing these standards. Businesses are not just saving money; they're also contributing to global efforts to combat climate change and preserve the planet for future generations.

## Employee Opportunities and Well-being

EcoChef certification isn't just an outward-facing badge to attract customers; it has a direct impact on the quality of life for employees working within the establishment. One of the pillars of EcoChef is energy efficiency, which often leads to the adoption of state-of-the-art kitchen technologies. This exposes employees to the latest equipment and best practices in the industry, thereby enriching their skill set and enhancing their employability. Furthermore, the certification's focus on innovation can create a culture of continuous learning and improvement, opening the door for employees to take on more responsibilities or even ascend to leadership roles within the organization.

The well-being of staff is often an overlooked aspect in busy commercial kitchens. EcoChef's focus on ergonomics, comfort, and indoor air quality is designed to change this. An improved working environment doesn't just boost employee morale; it also impacts their physical health. Ergonomically designed kitchens can reduce the physical strains commonly experienced in this profession, such as back pain or wrist issues. Improved ventilation and air quality can have far-reaching health benefits, reducing respiratory issues and providing a more comfortable, less stressful work environment. All of these factors contribute to greater job satisfaction, which in turn can lead to reduced staff turnover, a significant concern in the hospitality industry.

## Pioneering Innovation and Setting New Standards

EcoChef serves as a catalyst for groundbreaking innovation in the culinary sector. By encouraging creative endeavors that push the boundaries of existing sustainability measures, the program allows establishments to become trailblazers in ecological responsibility and culinary artistry. The introduction of a formal framework for such innovation ensures that the hospitality sector continues to evolve, setting new benchmarks for what can be achieved in sustainable practices.

In essence, EcoChef is not just about running a kitchen efficiently; it's about pioneering a holistic, sustainable approach to hospitality that benefits business owners, employees, guests, and most importantly, the planet. It sets the stage for a culinary future that harmonizes economic viability with ecological responsibility, impacting the hospitality sector in ways that will be felt for generations to come.

**In summary** EcoChef has set a precedent in the hospitality industry by meticulously focusing on the intertwining goals of environmental sustainability, employee well-being, and operational efficiency. However, it is just a steppingstone toward a more sustainable and equitable culinary landscape. As technologies evolve and environmental challenges become more urgent, the standards set by EcoChef today will likely be the baseline requirements of tomorrow. The certification encourages a culture of continuous improvement and innovation, setting the stage for future accreditation and sustainability initiatives to build upon its foundation.

The influence of EcoChef is likely to stretch beyond the boundaries of the hospitality industry, potentially inspiring similar movements in other sectors. As consumer awareness grows and sustainability becomes a non-negotiable aspect of business operations, certifications like EcoChef will continue to gain prominence. This opens avenues for the program to evolve, perhaps incorporating even more stringent criteria or branching into specialized certifications. The future is wide open, but the road ahead appears to be green and promising, thanks to pioneering initiatives like EcoChef.

## 5.8 The Impact of WELL Certification on the Hospitality Industry

In a landscape dominated by an increasing awareness of environmental and well-being issues, the WELL Building Standard (often referred to as WELL Certification) has emerged as a pivotal benchmark for health and wellness in the built environment. While the hospitality industry has long focused on guest satisfaction, the WELL Certification extends this philosophy to cover the holistic well-being of both guests and staff. In this section, we delve into the intricate facets of WELL Certification, examining its criteria, its relevance to the hospitality industry, and the broader implications for a sector so deeply tied to customer experience and employee satisfaction.

The integration of WELL Certification within the hospitality industry represents a paradigm shift, not just in construction and operational standards but also in organizational philosophy. By addressing various components like air and water quality, nourishment, light, fitness, comfort, and mind, this certification aims to create environments that enhance human health and well-being. This approach harmoniously aligns with the industry's core values, making it a crucial asset for future developments.

## What is WELL Certification?

WELL Certification is an evidence-based system for measuring, certifying, and monitoring the performance of building features that impact health and well-being. It goes beyond the traditional aspects of building certifications that focus mostly on environmental sustainability. WELL encompasses a broader view of health, addressing physical, emotional, and social wellness through design and operation.

While LEED certification is often more focused on environmental sustainability, WELL dives deeper into human-centric factors. Its criteria address elements that directly influence the well-being of occupants—such as air quality, noise, temperature, and lighting—making it particularly relevant to hospitality settings where guest experience is paramount.

## Criteria for WELL Certification

The WELL Building Standard is divided into seven key areas: air, water, nourishment, light, movement, thermal comfort, and mind. Each category is backed by scientific research and aimed at promoting holistic well-being. Hospitality establishments, like hotels and restaurants, can tailor these criteria to suit their unique settings.

For example, they can implement advanced water filtration systems, design interiors that facilitate natural lighting, or create menu options that encourage nourishing food choices.

To achieve certification, establishments must undergo rigorous testing and annual re-certification, ensuring they continually meet the ever-evolving wellness standards. This serves as both an assurance and a challenge for businesses in the hospitality industry, pushing them towards sustained commitments to holistic wellness.

## Importance in the Hospitality Industry

WELL Certification has become increasingly important in the hospitality industry as businesses strive to meet the rising demands for healthier and more sustainable environments. Given that consumers are becoming more health-conscious and environmentally aware, having a WELL Certification can provide a competitive edge. It serves as a mark of commitment to guest and employee wellness, potentially driving higher occupancy rates and customer loyalty.

Moreover, the focus on well-being also translates to employee satisfaction and productivity. In an industry with high turnover rates, creating a workplace that prioritizes employee health can be a significant advantage. A WELL-certified environment could attract quality talent and contribute to improved staff retention.

## Relation to Other Certifications

WELL Certification complements other sustainability and wellness initiatives like LEED, ENERGY STAR, and EcoChef. While each has a specific focus—be it environmental sustainability, energy efficiency, or culinary excellence—WELL bridges these elements by focusing on human health and well-being. In a sense, it completes the trifecta of sustainability, efficiency, and wellness that is increasingly becoming a gold standard in the hospitality industry.

Hospitality businesses that already have certifications like LEED or ENERGY STAR can find it easier to adapt to WELL standards, as some of the criteria overlap. This gives establishments an opportunity to be recognized for multiple dimensions of sustainability and wellness, making them more appealing to a broader range of consumers and stakeholders.

**The Future: Beyond WELL Certification**

While WELL Certification is a step forward in advancing the integration of health and well-being into built environments, it is just one milestone in the continuous journey toward comprehensive sustainability and wellness. Emerging technologies and evolving scientific understanding of well-being will only raise the bar for what can be achieved. Future versions of WELL Certification may include even more stringent criteria, perhaps leveraging advancements in smart technology to monitor and adapt environments in real-time.

As we move toward a future where well-being becomes a non-negotiable aspect of all industries, not just hospitality, the lessons learned from implementing WELL Certification will prove invaluable. This certification sets the stage for what could become a universal standard, influencing not just how buildings are constructed and operated, but how we fundamentally understand the relationship between environments and human health.

# 5.9 The Influence of ILFI on the Hospitality Industry

In the rapidly evolving landscape of sustainability and well-being, the International Living Future Institute (ILFI) stands as a transformative entity shaping the future of built environments. Particularly in the hospitality industry, where customer experience and sustainable practices are converging, ILFI's Living Building Challenge and other initiatives offer comprehensive frameworks for achieving an unprecedented level of ecological and social responsibility. This section explores the essence of ILFI, its frameworks like the Living Building Challenge, and its profound impact on the hospitality industry.

The introduction of ILFI's principles into the hospitality industry represents a monumental shift, not merely in structural design but in how hospitality entities think about their roles in both local and global ecosystems. ILFI goes beyond traditional sustainability by envisioning buildings as living, regenerative entities. This novel approach dovetails effectively with the hospitality industry's increasing commitment to offer more than just a service, but an experience that is deeply rooted in environmental and social sustainability.

**What is ILFI?**

The International Living Future Institute is an NGO committed to catalyzing a transformation toward communities that are socially just, culturally rich, and ecologically restorative. ILFI is best known for its Living Building Challenge, a rigorous sustainability certification program that goes beyond the usual 'sustainable' or 'green' labels to aspire for net-zero or even net-positive impacts on water, energy, and waste.

Understanding ILFI is essential for grasping the future of sustainability in the hospitality industry. Unlike other certifications that focus on reducing harm, ILFI's programs actively encourage positive contributions to local environments and communities. This human-centered and ecology-minded approach aligns well with the hospitality industry's evolving priorities, adding another layer of depth to sustainability efforts.

## Criteria for Living Building Challenge

The Living Building Challenge is an ambitious building certification program that lays down strict criteria for sustainability, based on seven performance areas, or 'Petals': Site, Water, Energy, Health & Happiness, Materials, Equity, and Beauty. Each Petal is subdivided into imperatives that set specific targets for building projects, encouraging them to go beyond mere sustainability towards a restorative and regenerative design.

For hospitality establishments, meeting these imperatives could mean an extensive overhaul of operations, from sourcing local and sustainable materials for construction to implementing waste management systems that not only reduce but also reuse waste. The implications are far-reaching and extend to how guests interact with spaces, how employees experience their workplace, and how the establishment impacts the local community and ecosystem.

## Importance in the Hospitality Industry

ILFI and the Living Building Challenge provide a framework that greatly amplifies the sustainability efforts in the hospitality industry.

Given the high consumer demand for sustainable and ethical practices, having an ILFI certification can be a unique selling point. Achieving the Living Building Challenge standards not only elevates a brand's reputation but also holds the potential to redefine what luxury and comfort mean in a resource-strained world.

Moreover, these standards help set a new norm for employee working conditions, covering everything from natural lighting to air quality. For an industry that often suffers from high employee turnover and low job satisfaction rates, creating an ILFI-compliant environment could be a strategic move in not just attracting but retaining talent.

## Relation to Other Certifications

ILFI's programs and certifications can either stand alone or work in conjunction with other environmental and well-being certifications like LEED, WELL, and EcoChef. What sets ILFI apart is its regenerative focus. While LEED may focus on environmental sustainability and WELL may aim at human health and comfort, ILFI synthesizes these objectives and adds an imperative for social justice and community well-being.

Hospitality businesses that are already committed to sustainability and employee well-being may find ILFI to be the next logical step in their sustainability journey. The Living Building Challenge and other ILFI programs offer an integrated approach to solving the many interconnected issues facing the industry today, making the establishment more appealing to both socially conscious guests and potential employees.

## The Future: Beyond ILFI

As ILFI and its Living Building Challenge evolve, we can expect even more stringent and comprehensive criteria aimed at encouraging restorative and regenerative projects. The hospitality industry will likely see more establishments striving for this gold standard of sustainability, especially as consumer awareness and demand for eco-friendly options continue to rise.

The importance of ILFI in shaping the future of the hospitality industry cannot be overstated. As we transition to a new paradigm that places equal emphasis on environmental, social, and human capital, ILFI provides the tools and vision to make this complex transition possible. It's more than a certification; it's a catalyst for change in the way we think about built environments and their potential to benefit both people and the planet.

## 5.10 The Role of BREEAM Certification in the Hospitality Industry

While the hospitality industry has seen an influx of sustainability certifications and initiatives, BREEAM (Building Research Establishment Environmental Assessment Method) remains one of the earliest and most widely used environmental assessment methods for buildings. Established in 1990 in the United Kingdom, BREEAM sets the standard for best practices in sustainable design, construction, and operation across various types of structures, including hotels and restaurants.

BREEAM offers a robust and comprehensive framework that intersects with the key concerns of the hospitality sector. Whether it's energy efficiency, waste management, or indoor environmental quality, BREEAM's diverse set of criteria provides a roadmap for achieving sustainability goals without sacrificing guest experience or operational efficiency.

## What is BREEAM?

BREEAM serves as a global framework, offering impartial third-party evaluations of sustainability efforts across various structures, communities, and infrastructure initiatives. In contrast to certain other certification programs that concentrate exclusively on environmental factors, BREEAM adopts a comprehensive approach that also encompasses economic and social sustainability elements.

In essence, BREEAM aims to mitigate the environmental impacts of buildings, enhancing the well-being of the people who live and work in them and encouraging economic viability. This comprehensive approach aligns well with the broader values and goals of the hospitality industry, which has begun to adopt a multifaceted perspective on sustainability that extends beyond environmental conservation to include guest satisfaction and employee well-being.

## Criteria for BREEAM Certification

BREEAM certification works on a point-based system, where a building project earns points for meeting certain criteria in categories like Energy, Health & Well-Being, Innovation, Land Use, Materials, Management, Pollution, Transport, Waste, and Water. The accumulated points then translate into one of the five BREEAM ratings: Pass, Good, Very Good, Excellent, and Outstanding.

For the hospitality industry, this allows for a flexible yet robust approach to sustainability. Hotels and other establishments can strategize their sustainability efforts based on the specific criteria that align best with their brand values and operational needs.

Whether focusing on energy-efficient HVAC systems or employee health programs, BREEAM's comprehensive criteria offer the opportunity for a customized approach to sustainability.

## Importance in the Hospitality Industry

Being BREEAM-certified brings immediate credibility to hospitality businesses in an increasingly eco-conscious market. A BREEAM certification is often viewed as a hallmark of commitment to environmental stewardship, social responsibility, and corporate ethics. This can translate into a competitive advantage, attracting guests who prioritize sustainability when choosing accommodation or dining options.

Furthermore, BREEAM's commitment to sustainability goes beyond mere environmental metrics to include economic and social sustainability. This holistic approach resonates well with the hospitality industry's broader objectives. Whether it's through energy savings, enhanced guest experiences, or improved employee working conditions, BREEAM can significantly contribute to the overall success and sustainability of hospitality enterprises.

## Relation to Other Certifications

While BREEAM shares some similarities with other certifications like LEED, WELL, EcoChef, and ILFI, it has its own unique attributes. For instance, BREEAM's longevity and widespread recognition, especially in Europe, provide it with a distinct brand cachet. BREEAM's broader scope, which encompasses not just environmental but also economic and social aspects of sustainability, makes it particularly suited for the multifaceted needs of the hospitality industry.

It's worth noting that hospitality businesses can opt for more than one certification, depending on their specific sustainability goals. While LEED might offer rigorous guidelines for energy efficiency and ILFI might push the boundaries with its focus on net-positive impacts, BREEAM provides a balanced, holistic framework that can complement these specialized approaches.

### The Future: Beyond BREEAM

As sustainability considerations continue to gain momentum, the BREEAM certification will likely evolve to incorporate even more stringent criteria, further pushing the boundaries of what is considered 'sustainable.' The hospitality industry can expect a growing alignment between customer demand for sustainable practices and the evolving standards set by certifications like BREEAM.

In the future landscape of the hospitality industry, BREEAM certification could become as fundamental as other industry standards. As we grapple with the pressing challenges of climate change, resource depletion, and social inequality, BREEAM's comprehensive approach to sustainability will remain crucial in guiding the hospitality industry towards a more responsible and sustainable future.

## 5.11 Summary: The Convergence of Certification & Sustainability in the Hospitality Industry

As we conclude this comprehensive dive into the realm of certifications and their impact on energy efficiency in the hospitality sector, several key insights emerge. Certifications like ENERGY STAR, LEED, EcoChef, WELL, ILFI, and BREEAM are not just badges of honor; they are critical frameworks that drive systemic changes, helping the industry transition towards more sustainable practices. Their influence extends beyond energy savings, impacting various aspects of the operational landscape from waste management to employee well-being, and from cost-saving to boosting market reputation.

ENERGY STAR set the groundwork for what is possible in terms of energy efficiency, paving the way for subsequent certifications that specialize in different facets of sustainability. For instance, LEED certification focuses on building design and operation, while EcoChef targets commercial kitchens and WELL is concerned with human health and well-being in the built environment. ILFI aims at creating a socially equitable, culturally rich, and ecologically restorative environment. BREEAM's holistic approach addresses economic, social, and environmental sustainability, offering a comprehensive certification that has international reach.

What binds these certifications together is the common goal of reducing the industry's carbon footprint and promoting energy efficiency, thereby directly mitigating the effects of climate change. It's important to remember that the hospitality industry is a significant consumer of energy and resources. Any reduction in energy consumption or waste translates to notable environmental and economic benefits. Moreover, the growing consumer demand for eco-friendly establishments has made these certifications not just desirable, but often essential for success in a competitive market.

As additional enterprises within the hospitality sector embrace these certification initiatives, they contribute not only to their own sustainable practices but also act as catalysts, propelling the whole industry toward a more accountable and eco-conscious future. These certifications serve as a blueprint for the effective integration of sustainability into business practices, highlighting how environmental concerns can coexist with, and even bolster, profitability, and customer satisfaction. In essence, the certifications discussed in this chapter are instruments of change, integral for steering the hospitality industry towards a sustainable, energy-efficient, and socially responsible future.

# Chapter 6

# Waste Reduction/Diversion and Recycling Strategies

In a world where environmental sustainability is an ever-increasing priority, waste reduction, diversion, and recycling have become critical components of responsible business practices. Whether you're managing a company, a municipality, or an individual household, adopting effective waste management strategies is essential for minimizing environmental impact, conserving resources, and reducing the strain on landfills.

Waste reduction involves rethinking our consumption patterns, diverting materials from landfills, and recycling valuable resources. It's a multifaceted approach that not only benefits the planet but can also result in substantial cost savings for businesses and communities alike.

## 6.1 Waste management systems: recycling, composting, and waste-to-energy technologies

As we delve into the intricate layers of the green industrial revolution, it becomes clear that waste management is not merely an operational requirement but a critical component of the sustainability equation. The hospitality industry, which often grapples with high levels of waste—especially in kitchen operations—stands to benefit enormously from advanced waste management strategies. In this light, this section explores integrated waste prevention & management systems that incorporate recycling, composting, and waste-to-energy technologies.

Recycling is one of the fundamental approaches to waste management that has received significant attention from various disciplines, including engineering and political science. By separating and collecting recyclable materials such as paper, plastic, and glass, establishments in the hospitality sector can divert these resources from landfills. Not only does this contribute to the conservation of valuable raw materials, but it also minimizes the ecological footprint of the business. ENERGY STAR and other certifications often have guidelines and benchmarks for effective recycling programs, making it easier for hotels and restaurants to adapt and implement these strategies.

When it comes to composting, both chefs and sustainability experts agree on its necessity and benefits. Organic waste—comprising of food scraps, plant materials, and biodegradable items—can be turned into nutrient-rich compost rather than ending up in a landfill. This practice aligns well with sustainable landscaping initiatives, eliminating the need for chemical fertilizers and further lowering the environmental impact. Composting not only minimizes waste but also enriches the soil, creating a win-win scenario for both the environment and the business.

Waste-to-energy technologies provide an innovative pathway for managing waste. Through methods like anaerobic digestion or incineration, non-recyclable waste can be transformed into renewable energy sources, such as electricity or heat. Engineers and architects often work in tandem to design and implement these systems, ensuring that they align with the overall sustainable goals of the establishment. This is particularly crucial in the hospitality industry, where the generation of sustainable energy can significantly reduce greenhouse gas emissions and operational costs.

By employing a comprehensive waste management strategy that integrates recycling, composting, and waste-to-energy technologies, the hospitality sector is positioned to drastically reduce waste, conserve resources, and contribute positively to broader sustainability goals. These strategies not only bolster the industry's commitment to a greener future but also offer operational benefits that enhance efficiency and cost-effectiveness. Thus, embracing these integrated waste management systems represents a pivotal step in aligning the hospitality industry with the overarching objectives of the green industrial revolution.

## 6.2  Strategies for Reducing Food Waste in Hospitality Operations

The global imperative of minimizing food waste finds a particularly poignant echo in the hospitality sector, which is a significant contributor to food waste due to its large-scale food preparation and service. As we seek to marry concepts of energy efficiency, sustainability, and responsible business practices, reducing food waste becomes a critical intersection of these themes. In this section, we will delve into various strategies that can drastically mitigate the industry's food waste dilemma while exploring how these practices align with certifications like ENERGY STAR and contribute to a more sustainable business model.

Menu planning is the chef's roadmap for achieving sustainability within the bounds of culinary artistry and guest satisfaction. Working autonomously, with farmers, or with a core team of hospitality professionals, chefs use their expertise to carefully craft menus and portion sizes that are attuned to both customer preferences and sustainability goals. Precision in these areas can substantially minimize food waste. By paying close attention to guests' dining behaviors, dietary needs, and feedback, chefs can continually refine their menus to ensure that what is being served aligns well with what is actually consumed, reducing both kitchen and plate waste. This customer-centric approach allows chefs to be stewards of sustainability, balancing the demands of fine dining with the pressing need for responsible resource management.

Effective inventory management is another cornerstone in the edifice of waste reduction. Engineered solutions, often involving software tools, can help monitor inventory levels and expiration dates. By doing so, businesses can ensure optimized food usage, minimizing the discard of excess or spoiled items. This approach not only leads to waste reduction but also translates into energy efficiency, as less energy is required to produce, store, and dispose of wasted food.

Training the staff is not just an operational necessity but a sustainability imperative. By educating kitchen and serving staff on proper food handling, storage, and portioning techniques, a considerable amount of food waste can be avoided during both preparation and service. Engaging employees in sustainability efforts can also have a ripple effect, instilling a broader culture of ecological responsibility throughout the organization. Various certifications focus on staff training as a measure of an establishment's commitment to sustainability.

Social responsibility also finds a role in food waste reduction through the donation of surplus food. Hotels and restaurants can collaborate with local charities, food banks, or shelters, converting potential waste into community welfare. Such initiatives not only minimize landfill use but also address the critical issue of food insecurity.

Complementing recycling and composting efforts outlined earlier, composting food scraps can close the loop on food waste. Collected food waste can be channeled into nutrient-rich soil amendments, which can then be used in landscaping or sold to local farms, creating a circular economy model. This is where the concept of waste diversion becomes an economic opportunity, aligning with broader sustainability initiatives like regenerative agriculture.

In conclusion, combating food waste in hospitality operations requires a multi-pronged, interdisciplinary approach. It brings management, staff, guests, and community members into a collaborative effort aimed at both environmental stewardship and operational efficiency. These practices not only reduce the industry's ecological footprint but also offer substantial cost savings, as every piece of wasted food equates to wasted resources and money. By embracing these methods, establishments in the hospitality industry underline their commitment to a sustainable future, aligning themselves effectively with the broader goals of the green industrial revolution.

## 6.3 Waste Diversion Strategies: A Hands-On Approach for Chefs & Hospitality Professionals

Waste diversion tactics are more than just a nod to recycling; they are central to the operations of a chef's kitchen and are crucial for any hospitality entity targeting sustainable practices. These methods aim to reduce the volume of waste that ends up in landfills and optimize the use of existing resources. Beginning with recycling programs, installing well-marked bins in kitchens and dining areas serves as a straightforward yet impactful step. Educating staff about the correct recycling procedures not only ensures compliance but also offers an opportunity to connect with guests by sharing the business's dedication to eco-friendly waste management.

Composting is another avenue where chefs play a critical role. By implementing composting systems for food scraps and biodegradable waste, kitchens can transform what would have been waste into valuable compost. This not only diverts organic material from landfills but also can provide rich soil for local gardens or farms, aligning with the larger goals of sustainable agriculture and soil health. In some cases, the compost can even be used in the establishment's own garden to grow herbs and vegetables, further closing the loop on waste.

The concept of reuse and upcycling holds untapped potential in the hospitality industry. Encouraging the use of reusable containers for to-go orders or refillable water bottles in guest rooms can drastically reduce the reliance on single-use plastics. In the kitchen, upcycling can take on creative forms—think turning vegetable scraps into stocks or transforming day-old bread into croutons or bread pudding. These efforts not only reduce waste but also spark innovation in the kitchen, leading to unique dishes that please guests while respecting the planet.

Waste-to-energy technologies offer a cutting-edge solution for waste that cannot be recycled or composted. These systems convert non-recyclable waste into renewable energy forms like electricity or heat. Although the initial investment may be significant, the long-term benefits include reduced reliance on fossil fuels and a more sustainable energy mix for the establishment.

Adopting these waste diversion strategies can make a substantial difference in reducing a hospitality business' environmental footprint. They fit within the framework of a circular economy, which strives to keep materials in use for as long as possible through reusing, recycling, and upcycling. Beyond the ecological benefits, these efforts enhance a brand's reputation. Eco-conscious consumers are more likely to frequent establishments that are proactive about waste management, and this sentiment often extends to the investor community as well. By integrating these waste diversion strategies, chefs, and hospitality professionals can lead the way in creating a more sustainable future for both their industry and the planet at large.

## 6.4 Sustainable procurement and packaging practices

In the hospitality industry, the roadmap to sustainability extends into the often-overlooked areas of procurement and packaging. These practices are crucial elements of a comprehensive approach to sustainability that looks beyond energy use and waste management. They encompass various initiatives designed to mitigate the environmental and social repercussions of the materials and products that the industry consumes.

The cornerstone of sustainable procurement is responsible sourcing. This goes beyond merely purchasing organic or fair-trade goods and delves into a more meticulous selection process. By opting for products with a lesser environmental toll—those crafted from renewable resources or manufactured through eco-conscious methods—hospitality businesses can take meaningful strides in resource conservation and footprint reduction. Ethical sourcing adds another layer to this, emphasizing fair labor conditions and promoting suppliers that prioritize both environmental and employee welfare.

The issue of packaging holds a considerable weight in the waste equation, particularly in the context of a chef's kitchen where bulk purchases are frequent. Hospitality entities can make significant reductions in waste by revising their packaging strategies. This could involve transitioning to recyclable or compostable materials, adopting minimalist packaging designs, or promoting the use of reusable containers. Such practices resonate well with a growing segment of guests who prefer greener packaging options, while also reducing the volume of waste sent to landfills.

The ripple effects of adopting sustainable procurement and packaging strategies extend beyond ecological benefits. They address the increasing consumer demand for ethical and sustainable operations, thereby expanding the customer base and building brand loyalty. By visibly committing to sustainability, businesses not only meet consumer expectations but also elevate the entire industry standard.

Another added advantage is the long-term cost-efficiency these practices can bring. While initial expenditures may be required to transition to more sustainable materials or vendors, the subsequent reduction in resource usage and waste management costs can generate operational savings over an extended period.

In summary, embracing sustainable procurement and packaging methods serves as a multipronged strategy that advances environmental responsibility, fulfills consumer expectations, and can positively impact the financial bottom line. By being proactive in these domains, hospitality businesses, from hotels to restaurants, can position themselves as leaders in the march towards a more sustainable and socially responsible industry.

## 6.5   Involving Chefs, Staff, & Guests in Sustainable Waste Management

Creating a culture of sustainability in hospitality—especially in the nerve center that is a chef's kitchen—relies heavily on the active involvement of both staff and guests. The key to building this culture is education and empowerment, allowing each stakeholder to understand their role and impact in sustainable waste management.

Staff training emerges as the backbone of this initiative, equipping culinary teams and other employees with the actionable know-how to enact meaningful changes. Training should focus on the specifics of waste management within the culinary context, such as proper food storage techniques, reducing food scraps during preparation, and correct procedures for recycling and composting. In the chef's kitchen, for example, culinary staff can learn how to repurpose food waste or how to minimize waste through precision cutting techniques.

Incorporating recycling and composting programs into daily operations can solidify the organization's commitment to waste reduction. The chef's kitchen, dining areas, and staff lounges should feature strategically placed, clearly labeled bins for recycling and composting. Explicit guidelines and periodic staff briefings can reinforce the correct sorting of recyclable and compostable materials, thereby optimizing the waste diversion strategy.

Guest involvement is another linchpin in the waste management chain. By offering clear, concise instructions on waste separation in guest rooms and common areas, businesses ensure that guests can contribute effectively to the establishment's sustainability goals. Simple signages in rooms about towel reuse or digital instructions on how to separate recyclables can make a significant difference.

Incentivizing sustainable practices amplifies guest participation. Offering tangible rewards, such as discounts or loyalty program points for opting for sustainable choices like towel and linen reuse, can motivate guests to engage in responsible consumption. This not only reduces laundry loads but also decreases water and energy usage, making it a win-win situation.

Raising awareness remains crucial. Strategically placed signs or digital information boards can be employed to educate guests about the establishment's sustainability initiatives. This has a dual purpose: first, to inform, and second, to inspire. The more guests understand about the waste management efforts of their chosen establishment, the more likely they are to respect and follow those efforts.

By actively engaging both staff and guests in a united front against waste, the hospitality industry creates fertile ground for sustainable practices. This not only elevates the guest experience—appealing particularly to the eco-conscious traveler—but also boosts staff morale and job satisfaction. A workforce that feels they are contributing to a larger purpose is generally more engaged and efficient.

In conclusion, by making waste management a shared responsibility between chefs, staff, and guests, hospitality businesses can make significant strides in reducing waste and fostering sustainability. This multi-stakeholder approach amplifies the industry's efforts in promoting responsible consumption, reducing environmental impact, and ultimately contributing to a more sustainable and eco-friendly future.

# CHAPTER 7

# WORKER HEALTH AND WELL-BEING IN THE HOSPITALITY INDUSTRY

The hospitality industry is renowned for its vibrant and dynamic atmosphere, welcoming guests from around the world. Behind the scenes, however, the well-being of the dedicated workforce that makes these experiences possible is a topic of paramount importance. From hotel staff and restaurant workers to event planners and tour guides, the demands of the hospitality sector can be physically and mentally taxing. As such, addressing worker health and well-being is not just a moral imperative but a strategic necessity.

## 7.1 The Symbiotic Relationship Between Worker Well-Being & Sustainable Hospitality

The importance of employee well-being in the hospitality sector takes on added urgency in the context of the green industrial revolution. This emerging paradigm shift is not just transforming technologies but is also closely interlinked with human factors like worker health. Providing a healthy and fulfilling work environment for chefs, servers, housekeepers, and other staff members goes beyond mere ethical obligations; it becomes a cornerstone for both business success and environmental sustainability. A workforce that is both healthy and happy not only elevates productivity but is also more likely to embrace and implement green practices. The synergy between worker well-being and environmental responsibility is vividly illustrated through the integration of ENERGY STAR and EcoChef-certified appliances, along with the implementation of green initiatives throughout kitchens and entire facilities. In this way, employee health and sustainability initiatives become interdependent aspects of a unified approach.

Drawing from interdisciplinary fields like architecture, engineering, and political science, the scope of worker well-being extends to well-designed, ergonomic workspaces and fair labor practices. Chefs, for instance, work in kitchens that are high-pressure environments requiring precision and speed. With advancements in green technology, modern kitchens can now incorporate ergonomically designed appliances and fixtures that reduce the physical strain on chefs, thereby decreasing occupational hazards. Such design considerations align with ENERGY STAR's certification, contributing to a kitchen's lower carbon footprint while also promoting worker well-being.

Flexible scheduling, an idea borne out of advanced workforce management algorithms and supported by political science research on work-life balance, can substantially contribute to mental well-being. Offering employees adequate rest periods and a work-life balance isn't just a decent practice; it's strategic. Research shows that well-rested employees are more creative and efficient, essential attributes in an industry requiring continual innovation to stay competitive.

Investing in ongoing training and professional development, such as sustainability certifications, helps build a well-rounded, committed workforce. In hospitality, where presentation and service are key, skilled employees can significantly elevate the guest experience. Their refined skills often translate into more sustainable practices, be it in food preparation, waste management, or customer service, thereby advancing the industry's contribution to the green industrial revolution.

Furthermore, preventing burnout is particularly crucial in hospitality, a sector notorious for its long hours and high-stress environments. Incorporating stress management techniques from psychology and promoting job rotation can add a layer of mental and emotional well-being. Engaging in stress-reduction measures such as mindfulness can lead to better decision-making and a happier work environment, fostering a sense of teamwork and camaraderie that's indispensable in service-based industries.

Employee assistance programs (EAPs) and holistic wellness initiatives, supported by data from the field of psychology, can offer mental health support, further lowering turnover rates and raising job satisfaction. These systems are not merely safety nets but proactive measures that validate employees, giving them a sense of belonging and a mentally stimulating environment, encouraging them to contribute their best.

To sum up, focusing on worker health and well-being isn't just an ethical choice but a sound business strategy that reinforces the sector's commitment to sustainability. By fostering a workplace that prizes its employees' physical and mental health, hospitality businesses not only attract top-tier talent but also catalyze their transition into eco-friendly practices, thereby fulfilling their role as responsible corporate citizens in the age of the green industrial revolution. This creates a win-win scenario that serves not just the industry and its employees but also sets a benchmark for environmental stewardship.

## 7.2 Understanding the unique challenges and risks faced by hospitality workers

Hospitality workers play a vital role in ensuring a positive and memorable experience for guests. However, they encounter unique challenges and risks in their daily tasks. The nature of the industry demands long and irregular working hours, making it difficult for workers to maintain a healthy work-life balance. Physically demanding tasks, such as lifting heavy objects and standing for extended periods, can lead to occupational injuries and musculoskeletal issues.

Exposure to hazards like slippery floors, hot surfaces, and potentially harmful cleaning chemicals poses safety risks for workers. Moreover, dealing with difficult and sometimes irate customers can take a toll on their mental well-being. The fast-paced and high-pressure environment in the hospitality sector can lead to stress and burnout, impacting both the physical and mental health of employees.

In addition to these challenges, workers may face issues related to job conditions and job security. Many hospitality workers earn low wages, which can lead to financial stress and hinder their quality of life. Job insecurity and limited career advancement opportunities can lead to job dissatisfaction and affect employee retention in the industry.

To address these challenges, employers in the hospitality sector must prioritize worker safety and well-being. Implementing proper training and providing personal protective equipment can reduce the risk of workplace accidents and injuries. Offering flexible work schedules and promoting work-life balance can help alleviate the stress of long and irregular working hours.

Employers can also invest in employee wellness programs to support the mental and emotional health of workers. These programs can include access to counseling services, stress management workshops, and resources for work-related burnout.

Improving wages and offering career development opportunities can enhance job satisfaction and motivate workers to stay in the industry. Providing a supportive and inclusive work environment that values and recognizes the contributions of employees can also contribute to higher job satisfaction and employee engagement.

Overall, understanding the unique challenges and risks faced by hospitality workers is essential for fostering a positive and healthy work environment. By implementing measures to prioritize worker safety, well-being, and job satisfaction, employers can create a supportive and fulfilling workplace that benefits both employees and the hospitality industry as a whole.

## 7.3 Navigating Occupational Hazards & Health Issues in the Hospitality Industry Amidst the Green Industrial Revolution

As the hospitality industry undergoes a transformational shift towards sustainability and greener practices, workers face a unique set of occupational hazards and health challenges that demand comprehensive solutions. Some of these risks are inherently tied to the work environment, while others have been exacerbated or modified by the industry's embrace of eco-friendly technologies and practices.

**Physical Hazards**

Physical hazards in the hospitality industry are diverse and often nuanced, influenced by the type of work and the specific environment. For instance, chefs and kitchen staff deal with hot surfaces, sharp knives, and open flames, elevating the risk of burns and cuts. Meanwhile, housekeeping and maintenance staff may be exposed to hazards like slippery floors, heavy lifting, and the use of electrical equipment.

In many cases, the adoption of greener technologies, such as energy-efficient lighting or non-slip, eco-friendly flooring, can mitigate some physical risks. However, transitioning to these newer technologies also requires an adjustment period during which employees need to become familiar with their operation and maintenance. To reduce the occurrence of physical hazards, employers can take proactive measures such as conducting regular safety audits, ensuring proper signage, and enforcing the use of personal protective equipment (PPE). Pairing these traditional safety measures with updated training on the new green technologies ensures that employees are well-equipped to handle both the conventional and emerging challenges of their roles.

## Heat Exposure

Heat exposure is a significant concern in the hospitality industry, especially for chefs and kitchen staff who work in close proximity to hot surfaces and equipment for extended periods. Conventional gas stoves and ovens can significantly contribute to high temperatures, exacerbating heat stress and increasing the risk of heat-related illnesses like heat exhaustion or heat stroke. Moreover, fossil-fueled equipment like gas stoves emits radiant heat that can't be exhausted out, adding another layer of risk to an already demanding environment.

Mitigating heat exposure involves several strategies, including improving ventilation systems, implementing regular rest breaks in cooler areas, and using moisture-wicking uniforms. Importantly, the transition away from fossil-fueled equipment like gas stoves to more sustainable and efficient options can drastically reduce radiant heat sources in the kitchen. This not only helps in cooling down the work environment but also aligns with the broader goals of the green industrial revolution. By incorporating appliances that are both energy-efficient and safer in terms of heat emission, employers contribute to both environmental sustainability and worker well-being.

## Mental and Emotional Well-being

The fast-paced and high-stress nature of the hospitality industry places unique emotional and psychological demands on its workers. Dealing with high customer expectations, irregular hours, and occasional verbal abuse can strain the mental health of employees, leading to heightened levels of stress, anxiety, and in extreme cases, burnout. The pressure to provide exceptional guest experiences can sometimes overshadow the need for staff well-being, leading to mental health struggles that can affect not only job performance but also personal lives.

Addressing these challenges requires a multi-faceted approach that goes beyond the confines of traditional occupational safety. Employers must prioritize mental and emotional support mechanisms, such as access to counseling services, stress management workshops, and resources to combat work-related burnout. By fostering a work culture that acknowledges and addresses mental health, the hospitality industry can not only improve employee satisfaction and retention but also align with the ethical and sustainability goals set forth in the green industrial revolution, which encompasses the overall well-being of the workforce.

## Ergonomic and Chemical Exposures

Ergonomic hazards are often overlooked but are an integral aspect of worker well-being in the hospitality sector, particularly in environments like kitchens where chefs and staff engage in repetitive movements and stand for extended periods. Poor ergonomic design can lead to work-related musculoskeletal disorders such as carpal tunnel syndrome, back pain, and chronic strain injuries. Investing in ergonomic solutions such as adjustable workstations, anti-fatigue mats, and training staff in proper lifting techniques can reduce these risks. With the advent of the green industrial revolution, there is also an increasing push towards ergonomic designs that are not only worker-friendly but environmentally sustainable, a synergy best exemplified by new kitchen technologies that are both efficient and ergonomically designed.

Chemical exposures, particularly in cleaning and maintenance tasks, present another set of challenges. Workers may come into contact with harmful substances present in cleaning supplies, which could lead to skin irritation or more severe respiratory issues. A move toward greener, less toxic cleaning supplies aligns with the broader goals of environmental stewardship set forth in the green industrial revolution. It's essential for employers to provide proper training on the use of these chemicals and to ensure well-ventilated workspaces. Personal Protective Equipment (PPE) like gloves and masks should be readily available to minimize risk.

## Shift Work and Sleep Disruption

Shift work and irregular hours are a common feature of the hospitality industry, contributing significantly to sleep disruptions and other health-related issues among workers. Unpredictable schedules can lead to circadian rhythm disruptions, adversely affecting sleep quality, and by extension, mental and physical well-being. These disruptions can lead to chronic fatigue, diminished cognitive abilities, and increased susceptibility to illnesses. Importantly, poor sleep patterns can undermine the effectiveness of any green initiatives by reducing staff's capacity to effectively manage and operate energy-efficient technologies, thus hindering the full realization of the green industrial revolution's benefits.

Employers can mitigate these adverse effects by implementing flexible scheduling and ensuring that workers have adequate time between shifts to rest and recuperate. Utilizing workforce management software can help businesses intelligently schedule staff to minimize sleep disruption. Moreover, providing resources like sleep hygiene workshops or wellness programs that include sleep management can go a long way in preserving the health and productivity of the workforce. With adequate rest, employees are better equipped to engage with and implement the green and efficient technologies that are transforming the hospitality sector.

## Solutions and Best Practices

In light of the multifaceted challenges and occupational hazards discussed, it's imperative for hospitality businesses to take a comprehensive approach to safeguard worker health and well-being, especially as the industry navigates the complexities of the green industrial revolution. The integration of ENERGY STAR-certified appliances and equipment not only aids in environmental sustainability but can also have indirect effects on worker health by minimizing heat exposure and emissions from radiant heat sources like gas stoves.

Physical hazards like slips and falls can be significantly reduced through robust training programs and by employing anti-slip mats and proper signage in high-risk areas. Enhanced safety protocols in eco-friendly kitchens, fitted with ENERGY STAR & EcoChef-certified appliances, will not only mitigate risks but also promote an eco-conscious working environment.

Addressing mental and emotional well-being is just as critical. Employers should invest in mental health programs that provide counseling services, stress management workshops, and mindfulness training, aligning these initiatives with the broader eco-friendly and sustainable practices of the establishment.

Ergonomic considerations, like proper furniture and equipment design, can reduce the risk of musculoskeletal issues. Chemical exposures can be minimized by switching to green cleaning supplies, thereby aligning worker safety with eco-friendly practices.

Lastly, leveraging smart scheduling tools can help in better workforce management, thereby reducing the negative impacts of shift work and sleep disruption on employees. These tools can be especially useful in optimizing staff rotation to ensure that employees are well-rested and thus more capable of contributing to the establishment's eco-friendly initiatives.

By implementing these solutions and best practices, businesses can achieve a win-win situation where employee well-being is maximized while minimizing the establishment's carbon footprint, aligning closely with the principles and objectives of the green industrial revolution.

## 7.4 Ergonomic Considerations in Sustainable Hospitality Workplaces

In the framework of the green industrial revolution, ergonomic considerations take on even more significance in the hospitality industry, synergizing with eco-friendly objectives to create safer and more sustainable work environments. Implementing ergonomic design is not just a matter of employee well-being; it's also a pathway to increased efficiency and reduced waste. For instance, well-designed, adjustable workstations allow staff to perform tasks more effectively, minimizing resource consumption and supporting the overall sustainability goals of the establishment. Similarly, ENERGY STAR and EcoChef-certified appliances can be integrated into these workstations, marrying ergonomics with environmental stewardship.

Ergonomic design goes beyond just physical hardware. Training programs should be implemented to educate staff on the importance of proper lifting techniques, posture awareness, and the optimal use of ergonomic tools and equipment. In the context of sustainability, these training programs can be aligned with broader eco-friendly practices, such as energy-efficient workflows or waste reduction techniques. By consciously merging ergonomic considerations with the principles of the green industrial revolution, hospitality businesses can elevate employee well-being, boost productivity, reduce turnover rates, and contribute to a healthier planet.

## Conclusion

This chapter has delved deeply into the essential yet often overlooked aspects of worker health and well-being in the hospitality industry. We've discussed the unique challenges and risks workers face, ranging from physical hazards like heat exposure and chemical use to emotional and mental stressors that are intensified by the fast-paced environment. Ergonomic considerations and the disruptive nature of shift work were also highlighted, underscoring their impact on employee health. The chapter posits that prioritizing employee well-being is not just an ethical responsibility but also a strategic one. Investments in ergonomics, mental health support, and better working conditions can contribute to a more engaged workforce and can align closely with broader environmental and sustainability goals. Both employee wellness and eco-friendliness are shown to be two sides of the same coin, reinforcing each other to create a more sustainable and successful hospitality industry.

# Chapter 8

# Overcoming Challenges in Green Technology Adoption

In today's rapidly evolving world, the adoption of green technology has emerged as a crucial imperative for societies worldwide. As we grapple with the escalating concerns surrounding climate change, resource depletion, and environmental degradation, the implementation of sustainable and eco-friendly solutions becomes paramount. However, navigating the path towards embracing green technology is not without its challenges. This journey is marked by multifaceted hurdles, ranging from financial constraints and technological barriers to resistance from established industries and inertia within society. This discourse delves into the intricate web of obstacles that hinder the widespread adoption of green technology, while simultaneously exploring potential strategies and innovations that can facilitate the transition towards a more sustainable future.

## 8.1 Barriers and Challenges to Implementing Green Technologies in the Hospitality Industry

Adopting green technologies in the hospitality sector is a crucial step toward aligning with the broader goals of the green industrial revolution. However, several challenges often inhibit this transformation, some of which are common across sectors while others are unique to the hospitality industry.

1. **Financial Hurdles:**

The initial cost of implementing greener technologies can be a significant roadblock, especially for small to medium-sized hospitality businesses. Whether it's transitioning to ENERGY STAR & EcoChef-certified kitchen appliances or installing solar panels, the upfront costs often overshadow the long-term financial and environmental gains. From an economic perspective, the perception of a delayed ROI (Return on Investment) often deters stakeholders from making the essential leap toward sustainability.

2. **Awareness and Knowledge Gaps**:

The hospitality industry is as much about service and experience as it is about operations. However, there exists a widespread lack of awareness and education regarding the benefits and practicalities of green technology adoption. This gap extends not just to business owners but also to architects and engineers responsible for designing eco-friendly spaces. Resistance to change frequently arises from a lack of understanding and skepticism about new approaches.

### 3. Technological Complexity:

As engineering and sustainability experts can attest, green technologies often require specialized knowledge for effective implementation and operation. Whether it's smart energy management systems or waste reduction technologies, the complexity can deter many in the hospitality sector who might not possess the technical know-how needed for successful deployment and maintenance.

### 4. Challenges in Retrofitting:

Many existing hospitality setups require significant retrofitting to accommodate green technologies. The architectural and engineering intricacies of retrofitting—ranging from spatial constraints to logistical nightmares—can make this an arduous process. Moreover, the retrofitting must often be conducted without disrupting ongoing operations, adding another layer of complexity.

### 5. Regulatory Hurdles:

Political science experts highlight the role of policy and regulation in green technology adoption. Sometimes, the legislative landscape can be more of an obstacle than an enabler, with cumbersome processes and a lack of clear incentives discouraging adoption. Uncertainty about future policies can also make hospitality businesses hesitant to invest in sustainable technologies.

### 6. Guest Expectations:

There exists a perceived tension between the adoption of green technologies and the maintenance of high service standards.

Concerns range from the myth that eco-friendly implies lesser quality to worries about how guests might respond to visible changes. The result is a cautious approach to technology adoption, driven by the fear of alienating clientele.

To navigate these challenges, a multifaceted strategy is essential. Collaboration among industry leaders, technology vendors, policymakers, and even the culinary experts who work directly with these technologies can help overcome barriers. By joining forces, these stakeholders can provide the financial strategies, educational resources, and policy support needed to accelerate the green revolution within the hospitality industry.

## 8.2   Strategies for Overcoming Barriers to Green Technology Adoption

The transition to green technologies in the hospitality sector is an urgent necessity in the era of climate change and environmental degradation. However, as outlined in the previous section, numerous barriers such as financial constraints, lack of awareness, technological complexities, and regulatory hurdles can stymie this transition. Overcoming these obstacles requires a multifaceted approach that involves multiple stakeholders, from hospitality business owners to architects, engineers, political scientists, and sustainability experts. This section aims to delve into the strategies that can help overcome these barriers, thereby facilitating the smooth adoption and implementation of green technologies in the hospitality industry.

Within this framework, we will explore financial incentives and funding mechanisms that can ease the economic burden of adopting sustainable technologies. We will also discuss educational initiatives aimed at building awareness and increasing the sector's capacity to adopt green technologies. Furthermore, we will touch upon the role of technological assistance and consultations, policy advocacy, and aligning sustainability efforts with guest expectations. By adopting a comprehensive strategy that addresses these issues, hospitality businesses can not only meet the pressing demands of environmental stewardship but also position themselves as leaders in the sustainable future of the industry.

## Financial Strategies for Overcoming Initial Costs

The high initial investment is often one of the most significant barriers to the adoption of green technologies in the hospitality sector. This issue is particularly prominent among small and medium-sized enterprises (SMEs), which may not have the financial resources to invest upfront. To overcome this hurdle, hospitality businesses can explore various financial incentives, including grants, tax breaks, and rebates offered by local or federal governments to offset costs. Additionally, some companies specialize in providing financial models such as leasing or power purchase agreements that can make the initial investment more manageable.

Architects and engineers can play a crucial role here by designing more cost-effective green solutions tailored for the hospitality sector. These solutions can often be modular or scalable, allowing businesses to implement them in stages, thus distributing the financial burden over time. By analyzing the long-term returns on investment (ROI) compared to traditional technologies, stakeholders can make a compelling case for the economic viability of green technologies.

## Awareness-Building and Educational Strategies

Limited awareness and knowledge can lead to skepticism and resistance to adopting sustainable practices. Educational campaigns that target not only hospitality managers, but also front-line staff can be incredibly effective in promoting understanding and acceptance of new technologies. Training programs conducted in collaboration with sustainability experts and chefs experienced in working with green technologies can provide practical insights into their daily use and maintenance.

Political science can offer strategies for policy advocacy, where industry professionals and businesses join forces to lobby for educational initiatives at a higher level, such as in hospitality and culinary schools. This integrated approach ensures the next generation of hospitality professionals will have sustainability ingrained in their training. Public awareness campaigns can also be useful in changing consumer perceptions, thereby addressing concerns about guest expectations not aligning with sustainable practices.

## Technological Solutions for Complexity and Retrofitting

The technological complexity of green solutions can often deter businesses from making the transition. Engineers and technical experts can streamline this process by offering consultation services to help these businesses understand what is required in terms of infrastructure, system integration, and ongoing maintenance. In particular, the expertise of engineers can be invaluable when it comes to retrofitting existing spaces, a commonly cited challenge for older establishments in the hospitality sector.

Architects specializing in sustainable design can also provide valuable insights into effective retrofitting strategies that minimize disruption and maximize efficiency. Partnerships between the hospitality sector and technology providers can facilitate the sharing of specialized skills and knowledge needed to successfully implement and utilize green technologies, making the technological transition smoother and more manageable.

## Policy Approaches and Collaborations

Regulatory hurdles often impact the speed at which green technologies are adopted. A collective approach involving policymakers, sustainability experts, and industry leaders can work towards shaping more favorable policies. Strategies can include lobbying for simplified permit processes for green technology adoption, or advocating for standards that are more aligned with the capabilities of existing green technologies.

Cross-industry collaborations can further help in overcoming barriers. Engineers, architects, chefs, and professionals from the political science and sustainability sectors can all contribute their expertise to develop holistic solutions that consider the multi-faceted challenges faced by the hospitality industry. Such collaborations can not only help individual businesses but can also set new industry standards, making it easier for others to follow suit.

By employing a multi-pronged strategy that considers financial, educational, technological, and policy-related aspects, the hospitality industry can significantly accelerate the adoption of green technologies, aligning itself more closely with the goals of the green industrial revolution.

## 8.3  Collaborations & Partnerships for Advancing Sustainable Innovation in the Hospitality Sector

Collaborations and partnerships serve as the backbone of sustainable innovation within the hospitality sector, a key player in the unfolding green industrial revolution. Forming strategic alliances with various stakeholders—from sustainability-focused organizations and industry associations to academic and research institutions—can provide a plethora of expertise and resources that individual businesses might not possess. These partnerships are crucial for sharing up-to-date information, best practices, and innovative solutions across the industry. They catalyze a culture of continuous advancement in sustainability, helping businesses stay ahead of emerging trends and incorporate cutting-edge green solutions effectively.

In the technological realm, partnerships with providers and suppliers specializing in eco-friendly solutions are invaluable. These can range from collaborations with engineers designing energy-efficient kitchen appliances to architects focused on sustainable building designs. Such partnerships make it easier to integrate innovative, energy-efficient technologies, waste management systems, or sustainable sourcing practices into daily operations. Leveraging the know-how of these specialized partners helps businesses navigate the challenges of implementing green technologies, ultimately bolstering their environmental performance metrics.

Engagement with local communities and non-governmental organizations (NGOs) adds another layer to the sustainability matrix. By entering into partnerships with these entities, the hospitality sector can not only adhere to sustainable tourism practices but also foster local cultural preservation and social initiatives. These collaborations strengthen communal ties, engender trust, and create a shared responsibility toward achieving sustainability goals, aligning closely with the rising demand for eco-tourism and socially responsible business practices.

Public-private collaborations further amplify the sector's ability to influence and adapt to regulatory landscapes. Partnering with governmental bodies allows the industry to contribute to the framing of policies that encourage sustainable practices. These engagements offer forums for knowledge exchange, consensus-building, and collective mobilization of resources. As chefs, political scientists, and sustainability experts converge in these platforms, the outcome is often a set of balanced, actionable policies that benefit both the industry and the environment.

Overall, these varied forms of collaboration play a vital role in accelerating the adoption of green technologies and sustainable practices within the hospitality sector. As consumer preferences increasingly lean towards eco-conscious choices, such collaborative approaches become a strategic imperative for businesses aiming to maintain competitiveness. The collective pooling of resources and expertise paves the way for a shared vision of a more sustainable, economically viable, and socially responsible industry.

## Conclusion

The adoption of green technologies in the hospitality sector is not without its challenges, from financial constraints and technical complexities to policy barriers and cultural resistance. However, as this chapter elucidates, these hurdles are far from insurmountable. Through a multifaceted approach that includes devising strategic financial plans, enhancing awareness, and adopting ergonomic best practices, the industry can gradually but effectively transition into a greener future. Partnerships and collaborations stand out as a cornerstone in this transformation, bringing together expertise from various fields like architecture, engineering, culinary arts, political science, and sustainability to drive collective action.

In closing, the green industrial revolution is poised to have a transformative impact on the hospitality sector, aligning it more closely with pressing global imperatives around climate change, public health, and social responsibility. This chapter provides a roadmap for navigating the complexities of this transition. As consumer preferences increasingly shift toward sustainability, the industry must keep pace through proactive adoption of green technologies and practices. Overcoming existing barriers and embracing collaborative strategies are key to ensuring the industry's sustainable and profitable evolution.

# Chapter 9

# Economic Benefits of Green Technologies

The dawn of the 21st century has brought with it a growing awareness of the environmental consequences of our industrial and technological endeavors. In response to the escalating concerns surrounding climate change, pollution, and resource scarcity, the world has witnessed a significant shift towards the adoption of green technologies. These innovations encompass a wide spectrum of solutions, from renewable energy sources to energy-efficient building designs and sustainable transportation options. While the primary aim of green technologies is to mitigate environmental harm, they also offer substantial economic benefits that are increasingly difficult to ignore. This exploration delves into the myriad economic advantages of embracing green technologies, illustrating how they not only safeguard our planet but also bolster economies and generate prosperity.

## 9.1 Exploring the economic advantages of adopting green technologies in the hospitality industry

The adoption of green technologies in the hospitality sector extends beyond environmental stewardship; it is an economically savvy strategy. Energy-efficient appliances and renewable energy systems, often developed in collaboration with engineers and architects, are designed to reduce energy consumption considerably, offering long-term financial benefits. Optimized water systems and waste management strategies can significantly lower operational costs. These technologies contribute to tangible economic gains by reducing utility bills, cutting down on maintenance costs, and enhancing the overall profitability of the enterprise. Moreover, improvements in resource efficiency usually demonstrate a favorable return on investment (ROI), mitigating the impact of initial setup costs.

Branding also plays a crucial role in the economic benefits of adopting green technologies. Establishments that commit to eco-friendly practices are more appealing to a growing segment of the consumer population. Chefs and culinary experts can advocate for sustainable sourcing and food waste reduction, enhancing the establishment's brand and aligning it with the expectations of environmentally conscious customers. This not only provides a competitive edge but may also translate into increased market share and revenue streams. On the policy front, governments are increasingly offering financial incentives, grants, and tax breaks, often lobbied for by sustainability experts and political scientists, to encourage green practices. This financial support can substantially offset the initial costs of implementing green technologies, making it even more economically viable for businesses to go green.

- **Case Study: Gas vs Induction**

The debate between induction and gas stoves presents an intriguing case study within the broader narrative of green technologies in the hospitality industry. Financially speaking, induction cooktops offer several economic advantages over their traditional gas counterparts, and the argument often begins with efficiency. Induction cooktops deliver approximately 90% of their energy to the food, compared to about 35% for gas stoves (although gas efficiency plumets when put to use). This increased energy efficiency translates directly to lower utility bills over time, contributing to a quicker return on investment (ROI).

Moreover, induction cooktops reduce the size and scope of expensive ventilation systems, as they don't produce combustion by-products like gas stoves do. This represents a significant saving on infrastructure and maintenance costs. In addition, induction cooktops are often easier and less costly to install, especially in spaces not already fitted with gas lines or in areas where gas prices are high. From an operational standpoint, induction stoves have faster cooking times and more precise temperature control, features that can enhance kitchen efficiency, reduce food waste, reduce chemical purchasing costs, and thereby contribute to the bottom line.

The move away from gas stoves also aligns with increasing regulatory trends aimed at reducing carbon footprints. Adopting induction technology can preemptively position a hospitality business favorably against potential future policies that might impose taxes or restrictions on greenhouse gas emissions. All these factors create a compelling financial argument for the adoption of induction stoves as part of a broader strategy to integrate green technologies in the hospitality sector.

In summary, the integration of green technologies in the hospitality industry serves as an economic lever as much as an environmental one. It offers a multi-faceted advantage that combines cost-effectiveness, brand enhancement, and market positioning, making it an integral part of a smart business strategy for a future-proof and resilient hospitality sector.

## 9.2  Return on investment (ROI) analysis and cost savings from energy and resource efficiency

When we talk about implementing green technologies and sustainable practices in the hospitality industry, it's crucial to understand that these initiatives aren't just morally responsible choices; they're financially sound decisions. ROI analysis serves as a pivotal decision-making tool, offering a quantitative measure of the fiscal advantages derived from adopting energy-efficient and resource-saving technologies. This financial calculus helps businesses understand how investments in sustainable initiatives, such as induction cooking technologies, LED lighting, or water-efficient fixtures, directly translate into utility cost savings and operational efficiency.

In practical terms, energy-saving technologies like LED lighting, occupancy sensors, and smart HVAC systems can result in significant utility bill reductions, thus speeding up ROI. The operational benefits extend beyond immediate energy savings. For example, water-saving fixtures and efficient irrigation systems can also reduce monthly utility bills and have a rapid payback period. Moreover, efficient waste management not only saves money but also may qualify the business for tax incentives or grants. This way, ROI analysis not only quantifies the direct benefits but also highlights the long-term value of sustainability measures.

Financial analytics empower stakeholders, from management to investors, by presenting them with data-driven evidence of the economic viability of sustainable practices. This becomes a strong selling point, especially when these measures also resonate with consumer expectations around sustainability, possibly driving increased revenue. Additionally, ROI analysis helps strategically prioritize sustainability efforts. Initiatives yielding higher ROI can be implemented first, making the most of limited resources.

Ultimately, ROI serves as a cornerstone metric for driving sustainability in the hospitality sector. By enabling businesses to quantify the financial benefits of green technologies and practices, ROI analysis encourages more extensive adoption across the industry. Thus, a data-informed approach to sustainability doesn't just make ecological sense; it also promotes economic resilience, creating a symbiotic relationship between businesses, consumers, and the planet.

## 9.3 Brand enhancement and market positioning through sustainable practices

As we move further into the era of the Green Industrial Revolution, the interplay between sustainability and brand value becomes increasingly consequential. In the hospitality sector, particularly for establishments focusing heavily on culinary services, adopting sustainable technologies and practices offers more than just environmental stewardship. It enriches brand identity, thereby creating an avenue for differentiation in an often-crowded marketplace. Hospitality businesses that incorporate sustainability into their ethos are perceived as leaders in social and environmental responsibility, a characteristic that holds weight with today's discerning consumers.

Aligning eco-conscious consumer values can translate into tangible economic benefits through increased customer loyalty and market share. The shift toward greener kitchen technologies, like induction stoves over gas alternatives, not only provides a compelling narrative but also demonstrates a meaningful commitment to health and environmental betterment. Such alignment can captivate customers who seek to make responsible choices, thereby fostering long-term brand loyalty. The incorporation of energy and water-efficient appliances, waste management protocols, and even partnerships with local, sustainable food suppliers can serve as touch points that build a rich, positive brand narrative.

Transparency in communication remains key to leveraging sustainable practices for brand enhancement. Narrating the story—not just of the journey toward sustainability but also of its positive impact—can create emotional connections with consumers. Whether it's through digital platforms or direct customer engagement, hospitality businesses should strive to share their sustainability milestones and future goals. The key here is to make this storytelling resonate across the multiple disciplines that feed into the hospitality industry—from architecture and engineering that make sustainability feasible, to culinary practices that make it delicious.

Additionally, an authentic commitment to sustainability can broaden the scope of strategic partnerships and open doors to new markets that are sustainability centric. Given the interdisciplinary nature of sustainable practices—spanning fields such as engineering, political science, and culinary arts—these partnerships can offer multifaceted advantages that can significantly elevate a brand's market position.

In summary, sustainable practices in the hospitality industry have moved beyond being just a trend or a public relations strategy. They are a comprehensive value proposition that can significantly enhance brand equity and market positioning. By thoughtfully embracing these practices, businesses are not just safeguarding the environment but are also crafting a compelling market identity, potentially increasing their share in a consumer landscape that is becoming progressively eco-conscious.

## Conclusion

This chapter illuminates the multifaceted economic advantages of adopting green technologies in the hospitality industry, particularly within the context of kitchen operations. From substantial cost savings and impressive return on investments to meaningful brand enhancement, the benefits are both tangible and transformative. Sustainable practices are not just ethical choices but are increasingly revealed to be astute business decisions as well. Through a confluence of engineering innovations, culinary expertise, political incentives, and sustainable management practices, the hospitality sector has the potential to be at the forefront of the Green Industrial Revolution.

As we have delved into the economic advantages, ROI considerations, and brand value augmentations, it becomes evident that the wave of green technology is not a fleeting trend but a paradigm shift that is reshaping the hospitality industry. In an ever-more competitive and resource-constrained world, adapting to this shift is not just advisable but essential. Ultimately, the push toward sustainability is an all-encompassing movement that benefits businesses, consumers, and the planet. For hospitality businesses keen on long-term success and relevance, going green is not just an option; it's an imperative.

# CHAPTER 10

# POLICY AND REGULATIONS DRIVING GREEN REVOLUTION

The emerging green industrial revolution is not solely a product of technological innovation; it is equally shaped by the national and international policies that govern our approach to energy, resource management, and sustainability. As the hospitality industry undergoes its green transformation, understanding the policy landscape becomes crucial for both adoption and adaptation. This chapter aims to provide an in-depth look into the policies and regulatory frameworks that drive the adoption of green technologies and sustainable practices in the hospitality industry.

## 10.1 Overview of U.S. National Policies Promoting Green Technologies and Sustainability

From landmark legislation like the Clean Air Act to international commitments such as the Paris Agreement, these policies not only set the standards but also offer incentives that make green adoption economically viable. By examining these policies through an interdisciplinary lens that encompasses perspectives from architects, engineers, chefs, political scientists, and sustainability experts, this chapter will enable you to appreciate how policymaking affects practical decisions in the hospitality industry. Whether you're considering switching to energy-efficient kitchen appliances or implementing a comprehensive waste management system, the regulations discussed here will offer invaluable context and guidance.

## National Policies: A Regulatory Push towards a Greener Future

In the United States, an evolving tapestry of national policies, regulations, and executive orders contributes to shaping the landscape of green technologies and sustainability. One of the cornerstone policies is the Clean Air Act, initially enacted in 1963 and periodically updated. This seminal legislation has spurred industries, including the hospitality sector, to adopt technologies that significantly cut down on harmful emissions. As a corollary, chefs and engineers have collaborated to develop kitchen appliances, like induction cooktops, which emit fewer pollutants than traditional gas stoves.

The Clean Water Act of 1972 and the Energy Policy Act, with its iterations in 1992, 2005, and 2007, further serve to incentivize sustainable practices across various industries. The Environmental Protection Agency (EPA) takes the helm in ensuring that these laws are adequately implemented. Through various incentives, tax credits, and penalties, the EPA encourages businesses to transition toward greener practices. This is especially relevant in the hospitality sector, where issues like water waste can be combated through better engineering solutions and design choices by architects specialized in sustainable practices.

## International Commitments and New Directions: The Global Stage

On the international front, the United States has shown its commitment to curbing climate change through its participation in global pacts like the Paris Agreement. The Agreement, widely recognized as a groundbreaking international endeavor, targets reducing greenhouse gas emissions to keep global warming under 2 degrees Celsius above pre-industrial levels. This global focus has ripple effects on domestic industries, including hospitality, compelling them to align with international standards of sustainability.

Moreover, President Biden's executive order, as part of the Major Economies Forum on Energy and Climate, aims to catalyze global climate action. This directive highlights the necessity for sector-specific approaches, including innovations in hospitality to reduce carbon footprints significantly. It encourages inter-sectoral collaborations, providing a space for professionals from various fields such as political science, engineering, and sustainability to work towards common goals.

## State-Level Initiatives and Beyond: The Localized Effort

Beyond national mandates, individual states have taken the lead in pursuing more localized sustainability goals. Renewable Portfolio Standards are commonly implemented, mandating that a specific percentage of electricity be sourced from renewable energies. Tax incentives and grants at the state level further motivate businesses, big and small, to adopt greener technologies.

**In Summary**

National and international policies, along with state initiatives, provide a comprehensive regulatory framework that incentivizes the adoption of green technologies and sustainable practices. This not only serves to protect the environment but also offers a blueprint for businesses in the hospitality sector to follow. By understanding these policies and leveraging the incentives they offer, the industry can make informed decisions that contribute to a greener future, consistent with both domestic and global sustainability objectives.

## 10.2 Overview of International Policies Promoting Green Technologies and Sustainability

Global efforts to combat climate change have catalyzed a slew of policies and regulations, fostering a sustainable and low-carbon future. Within the European Union, a key international player in sustainability initiatives, the Green Deal serves as a roadmap for making the EU's economy sustainable. This encompasses everything from decarbonizing the energy sector to investing in innovative technologies and promoting energy efficiency. The Paris Agreement, ratified by many countries globally, including the EU and the U.S., also serves as a cornerstone in international policy. It sets targets for reducing greenhouse gas emissions and aims to limit global warming to well below 2 degrees Celsius above pre-industrial levels. For the hospitality sector, these global frameworks provide a roadmap for adopting green practices and reducing carbon footprints.

## Specific International Policies Aimed at Decarbonization

Let's delve deeper into the specific policies that various European countries have enacted to accelerate the shift away from fossil fuels, with applications extending to sectors including hospitality.

*Austria*: The country has put forth ambitious goals, declaring that no gas heating will be allowed in new construction after 2023. Furthermore, no fossil heating systems will be replaced after 2035, with a complete phase-out of all fossil fuel heating targeted for 2040. For the hospitality industry, this necessitates a decisive pivot toward greener alternatives like induction heating technologies, not just for compliance but also for long-term operational efficiency.

*European Union*: The EU, as part of its broader Green Deal initiative, has mandated that there will be no more subsidies for fossil fuel boilers after 2026. This policy is particularly consequential for hospitality businesses, who must now seriously consider alternative, sustainable heating and energy solutions to be eligible for any form of subsidy.

*Zurich, Switzerland*: The city has taken a firm stance against fossil fuel-based heating systems. Starting 2025, no gas or oil heating systems can be installed in new buildings, and these must be entirely phased out in existing buildings by 2035. This presents a significant shift for the Swiss hospitality sector, which is notable given Switzerland's reputation as a global hospitality hub.

*The Netherlands*: The country has initiated a phased approach to eliminate fossil heating, requiring heat pumps (hybrid options are allowed) by 2026. Each of its 355 municipalities has been mandated to draft a plan by the end of 2021 that outlines the replacement of

100% of natural gas used for heat with low-carbon alternatives by 2050. This policy encourages a broad sectoral shift, affecting not just households but also commercial establishments like hotels and restaurants.

*Ireland*: While not specifically focused on electrification, Ireland has launched a comprehensive program aimed at facilitating energy upgrades for 500,000 homes by 2030. This program is expected to extend to the hospitality industry, offering financial incentives to make energy-efficient upgrades, including the adoption of green heating and cooking technologies.

*China*: Their 14th Five-Year Plan underscores a strategic shift toward environmental sustainability and low-carbon development. The comprehensive policy framework prioritizes green development and aims to hit peak carbon dioxide emissions before the year 2030, with a long-term goal of achieving carbon neutrality by 2060. What makes this plan particularly noteworthy for sectors like hospitality is its emphasis on improving energy efficiency in traditionally resource-intensive industries. The Chinese government is increasingly recognizing the substantial carbon footprint of the hospitality sector, which includes energy use for heating, cooling, and food preparation. As such, the 14th Five-Year Plan includes targeted commitments to incentivize and implement energy-efficient practices within this sector. These commitments not only offer a blueprint for future technological adoption but also reflect the changing consumer attitudes toward sustainability, both within China and in its interactions with the global tourism industry.

*Japan*: They have put forth an ambitious agenda known as the "Green Growth Strategy through Achieving Carbon Neutrality by 2050." This strategy reflects a holistic approach that merges economic advancement with environmental stewardship. The underlying premise is to transition toward a green economy that simultaneously stimulates economic growth while minimizing environmental degradation. The hospitality industry, a significant part of Japan's service sector, is included in this vision. The strategy aims to usher in a new era of technological innovations, from energy-efficient appliances in hotel kitchens to intelligent HVAC systems that optimize energy use across facilities. By aligning economic incentives with sustainability goals, Japan's Green Growth Strategy serves as a comprehensive roadmap for business sectors—including hospitality—to adopt practices that are both economically beneficial and environmentally responsible. The strategy signals a larger trend that does not see economic growth and environmental protection as mutually exclusive but rather aims to integrate them into a unified national agenda.

*South Korea*: The South Korean Green New Deal aims to transform the country into a low-carbon economy, investing in renewable energy, green infrastructure, and promoting electric vehicles. In the Southern Hemisphere, countries like Australia and New Zealand are increasingly looking at renewable energy solutions, including wind and solar, to reduce their carbon footprints. Their policies often include grants or subsidies for businesses, including those in the hospitality sector, to transition away from fossil fuels.

*Africa*: Countries in Africa, including Kenya and Morocco, are focusing on both mitigation and adaptation strategies. Renewable energy projects like solar and wind farms are popping up across the continent, subsidized by both national and international funding. Morocco has even set an ambitious goal to generate 52% of its electricity from renewable sources by 2030, a target that also influences sustainability policies within its burgeoning tourism and hospitality sector.

In summary, the growing tapestry of international policies geared towards sustainability underscores a global, collaborative drive to address climate change. These policies, each tailored to the unique challenges and opportunities within their jurisdictions, offer a rich set of blueprints for transitioning to a more sustainable future. For the hospitality sector, this represents a critical juncture where compliance with regulations intersects with consumer demand for environmentally responsible practices. Across professions—from architects and engineers to chefs and political scientists—the message is clear: sustainability is not an optional add-on but a central tenet that needs to be woven into the fabric of business operations and professional responsibilities.

## 10.3 Understanding Regulatory Frameworks and Incentives: Navigating the Path to Green Hospitality

Navigating the labyrinth of regulatory frameworks and incentives is paramount for hospitality businesses committed to incorporating sustainability into their operations. Regulatory frameworks form an intricate matrix of laws, guidelines, and standards that steer companies toward environmental stewardship. These cover a range of issues from stringent energy efficiency mandates—like phasing out traditional gas-powered stoves in favor of induction cooking—to comprehensive waste management protocols and responsible water consumption guidelines.

Compliance isn't merely a matter of fulfilling legal obligations; it is about aligning business operations with broader global and local sustainability objectives. Proficiency in these frameworks empowers businesses to proactively implement green practices, which is essential not only for complying with current laws but also for anticipating future regulations. A multidisciplinary approach involving insights from architects, engineers, chefs, and political scientists can further help in this nuanced transition, ensuring that the application of regulations is both effective and innovative.

Financial and reputational incentives serve as catalysts in this green transition. Various national and international programs offer monetary benefits like tax rebates, grants, or reduced rates on loans for eco-friendly improvements. Certifications such as LEED (Leadership in Energy and Environmental Design) or the Green Key not only lend credibility but also position the business advantageously in a marketplace where consumers increasingly opt for environmentally responsible choices.

The initial costs of adopting sustainable practices are often offset by these incentives, making the transition not just an ethical obligation but a financially prudent move. Moreover, the long-term cost benefits are substantial, ranging from savings on utility bills due to energy-efficient practices to reduced waste management costs. These financial perks can be seen as aligned with President Biden's executive order to promote global climate action, creating a favorable environment for industries to make the shift towards sustainability.

To encapsulate, understanding and leveraging the existing regulatory frameworks and incentives is a strategic imperative for hospitality businesses. These tools not only facilitate compliance but also offer a roadmap for businesses to engrain sustainability into their core operational ethos. In a rapidly changing global landscape, where environmental considerations are becoming integral to consumer choice and policy directives, adapting to these green imperatives is not just wise but essential for long-term viability.

## 10.4 Case Studies on Successful Policy Implementations and Their Transformative Impacts

As we delve deeper into the topic of policy frameworks and their role in promoting sustainability, it's instructive to examine real-world case studies that have successfully implemented these policies. These cases are not merely academic exercises; they provide tangible evidence of how thoughtful policymaking can bring about substantial change in both environmental sustainability and economic vitality. From state-level renewable energy mandates to city-wide zero waste strategies, the following examples serve as illuminating illustrations of how policy interventions can foster sustainability across multiple sectors, including the hospitality industry.

- **Case Study 1: California's Renewable Portfolio Standard (RPS)**

California's Renewable Portfolio Standard (RPS) serves as an exemplary initiative that mandates utilities to derive a specific percentage of their electricity from renewable sources. This policy has catalyzed a surge in renewable energy production, enticing investments and stimulating job creation in the green energy sector. By successfully achieving its 2020 target of sourcing 33% electricity from renewables, California has set a precedent not just for reducing carbon emissions but also for stimulating economic growth in green sectors, aligning perfectly with the global transition to sustainability.

- **Case Study 2: New York City's Energy Efficiency Programs**

New York City's various energy efficiency initiatives underscore the possibilities of city-wide policy implementation. Particularly noteworthy is the NYC Carbon Challenge, which engages universities, hospitals, and commercial buildings in a voluntary commitment to slash their carbon emissions. Participants have already made substantial cuts in carbon emissions, simultaneously benefiting from marked reductions in energy costs, an especially pertinent lesson for the hospitality sector aiming to achieve sustainability without sacrificing profitability.

- **Case Study 3: European Union Emission Trading System (EU ETS)**

The EU ETS stands as the world's most expansive cap-and-trade system, targeting industrial sectors' greenhouse gas emissions. This market-based approach has successfully driven down emissions across member countries, especially in the power generation sector. Apart from mitigating environmental impacts, the EU ETS has spurred innovation in low-carbon solutions and provided economic growth opportunities, making it a role model for integrating market mechanisms in environmental policy.

- **Case Study 4: Massachusetts' Green Communities Act**

Initiated in 2008, Massachusetts' Green Communities Act has incentivized cities and towns within the state to implement energy-efficient projects and sustainable practices. With funding and incentives as motivators, over 240 communities have adopted the 'Green Community' label, significantly diminishing the state's carbon footprint. This policy has also led to economic invigoration through green job creation and has attracted investments in clean energy, making it a standout example of how legislative action can drive sustainable development at a local level.

- **Case Study 5: Seattle's Zero Waste Strategy**

Seattle's Zero Waste Strategy is an ambitious policy aimed at achieving zero landfill waste by encouraging recycling and composting. The city's hospitality industry, among other sectors, is pivotal in this endeavor. Remarkably, Seattle has already hit a diversion rate of over 60%, thereby minimizing waste sent to landfills. This pioneering approach has positioned Seattle as a thought leader in waste management and circular economy practices, influencing other cities to adopt similar sustainability roadmaps.

In summary, these case studies exemplify the transformative potential of well-crafted policies. They demonstrate that regulatory frameworks and incentives can be highly effective tools for driving sustainable practices across sectors, including hospitality. These real-world examples offer actionable insights into creating a harmonious balance between environmental responsibility and economic prosperity, thereby shaping a more sustainable future.

# Conclusion

It's clear that the journey towards sustainability in the hospitality sector is both a global and a local endeavor, shaped by a complex web of regulatory frameworks, innovative technologies, and societal expectations. From outlining the key drivers of sustainability and examining the role of digital technologies, to delving into international policies and real-world case studies, we've seen that the sector has numerous tools and strategies at its disposal. These mechanisms not only help in compliance with evolving regulations but also offer avenues for cost-saving, brand differentiation, and meeting the increasingly eco-conscious consumer demand.

The mosaic of international policies and case studies underscores the reality that there is no one-size-fits-all approach to sustainability. Each country, state, and even municipality is crafting its unique pathway, offering a rich tapestry of lessons that can be adapted and applied in various contexts. For industry professionals, whether they are architects, engineers, chefs, or policy analysts, the call to action is clear: Sustainability must be integrated into the very core of business strategies and operations. As we move forward in an era increasingly defined by climate change and environmental degradation, the imperatives of sustainability are not just ethical or regulatory, but existential.

# Chapter 11
# Case Studies: Successful Green Transformations in Hospitality

In the realm of modern hospitality, a remarkable transformation is underway. The industry, often synonymous with opulence and extravagance, is increasingly embracing the principles of sustainability and environmental consciousness. As travelers become more environmentally aware and conscious of their ecological footprint, hotels and resorts are recognizing the need for a paradigm shift. This shift is not merely a response to consumer demand but also a strategic decision driven by the realization that sustainability can be both environmentally responsible and economically profitable. In this exploration, we delve into case studies that showcase successful green transformations within the hospitality sector, illuminating the ways in which forward-thinking establishments are not only reducing their impact on the planet but also redefining luxury and customer experience.

## 11.1 Examining Real-World Examples of Hospitality's Embracing of Green Technologies

As we navigate through this pivotal chapter, the emphasis is on practical applications. We aim to translate the theoretical frameworks, policies, and technologies discussed in previous sections into actionable insights. By investigating concrete case studies from hotels, resorts, and restaurants that have successfully adopted green technologies, we intend to extract valuable lessons and best practices. These cases will be enriched by the perspectives of professionals from various disciplines such as architects, engineers, chefs, political scientists, and sustainability experts.

- **Chatham University's Eden Hall Campus**

As the world's first fully self-sustained university campus, boasting America's first all-electric campus kitchen, Chatham University's Eden Hall Campus stands as a paragon of sustainable hospitality education. The campus integrates green technologies in its kitchen and dining facilities, thereby creating a real-world laboratory where students can learn best practices in sustainable hospitality.

Notably, the Eden Hall Campus showcases sustainable architecture and design principles in its buildings, including the utilization of energy-efficient materials and renewable energy systems like solar panels and a geo-exchange loop. As such, it provides a comprehensive model for sustainable hospitality, right from construction to daily operations.

- **Google's Bayview Campus**

Google's Bayview Campus, although not a traditional hospitality entity, provides invaluable lessons for large-scale food service operations. The campus kitchens are designed with cutting-edge energy-efficient appliances and advanced waste management systems that could easily be adopted by large hotels or resorts.

Beyond their kitchen operations, Google's Bayview Campus integrates smart building technologies and energy-efficient design in its dining facilities. The campus serves as a case study in how environmental sustainability and operational efficiency can co-exist, even in large-scale, high-demand environments.

- **Microsoft's Global Headquarters**

Microsoft's campus in Redmond, Washington, stands as a testament to what corporate commitment to sustainability can achieve. The campus includes everything from green roofs to all-electric energy-efficient kitchen appliances in its dining facilities. By adopting these features, Microsoft not only minimizes its own environmental footprint but also sets an example for the hospitality sector.

Microsoft's approach to sustainability also extends to its supply chain. It aims to procure food and other supplies from sustainable sources, thereby extending its eco-friendly practices beyond the boundaries of the corporate campus. This demonstrates how a comprehensive, systems-level approach to sustainability can result in meaningful change, offering valuable lessons for the hospitality industry.

- **NOMA**

Based in Copenhagen and often hailed as the world's best restaurant, NOMA has successfully bridged the gap between culinary innovation and environmental sustainability. Boasting a fully electrified kitchen and featuring state-of-the-art, energy-efficient appliances, NOMA set new standards for how gourmet cuisine and sustainability can coexist. This commitment has significantly lessened the restaurant's environmental impact, positioning NOMA as a shining example of what can be achieved in sustainable fine dining without sacrificing quality.

NOMA has further deepened its commitment to sustainability by prioritizing local sourcing for its diverse range of ingredients. This not only fortifies local economies but also minimizes emissions resulting from transportation. By seamlessly weaving together a plethora of green practices—from responsible sourcing to energy efficiency—NOMA stands as a compelling case study in comprehensive environmental stewardship. Its journey offers critical insights for any restaurant aiming to balance culinary ambitions with a sustainable ethos.

- **Hilton Hotels**

Hilton Hotels has moved well beyond rudimentary green practices to become a leader in sustainable hospitality. The company has invested heavily in smart technology, utilizing LED lighting and intelligent HVAC systems to cut down energy consumption drastically. They also employ energy management systems that allow for real-time monitoring and adjustments, enhancing overall energy efficiency.

Moreover, Hilton is forward-looking in its energy sourcing. The company has invested in on-site renewable energy production facilities, including solar panels and geothermal systems. Such investments not only help reduce the carbon footprint but also provide a hedge against fluctuating energy prices, marking a comprehensive strategy that aligns environmental stewardship with business sustainability.

- **Marriott International**

Marriott's "Serve 360: Doing Good in Every Direction" is not just a program but a philosophy that integrates sustainability into the company's DNA. It involves green technologies ranging from energy-efficient lighting and smart thermostats to water-saving fixtures and advanced waste management. By focusing on multiple aspects of sustainability, they can tackle the environmental issues from several angles.

In addition to their technology adoption, Marriott has set clearly defined, ambitious goals to reduce water and energy consumption and lower their carbon emissions. Their approach is data-driven, employing metrics and key performance indicators to measure and drive sustainability performance across their various properties, demonstrating a commitment that goes beyond mere compliance.

- **Scandic Hotels**

Scandic Hotels, a leading hospitality name in the Nordic region, has consistently won accolades for its green initiatives. Their environmental efforts extend from energy-efficient lighting and climate control systems to advanced waste management procedures. They aim for operational excellence by employing modern technologies, and their commitment has set them apart in the industry.

As a pioneer in corporate responsibility, Scandic also aims for carbon neutrality in their operations. Their long-term objectives include significant reductions in energy and water consumption across all their properties. They believe that achieving these ambitious targets is not just good for the planet but also a compelling business strategy that aligns with consumer demand for responsible travel options.

By examining these case studies, it is clear that the adoption of green technologies in the hospitality sector is both a business imperative and an environmental necessity. The strategies and practices of these pioneering organizations offer a rich tapestry of insights that can guide others in the hospitality sector. They prove that with the right approach and technologies, sustainability is not just a buzzword but a practical reality that

## 11.2 Lessons Learned & Best Practices from Sustainable Hotels, Resorts, & Restaurants

As we delve deeper into the evolving realm of sustainable hospitality, it's crucial to extract actionable insights from the endeavors of pioneers in this space. This section presents key lessons learned and best practices that have been successfully implemented by leading hotels, resorts, and restaurants worldwide. While the insights gathered here are by no means exhaustive, they serve as a robust starting point for hospitality businesses looking to navigate the complex journey toward sustainability. This is an interdisciplinary endeavor, requiring insights from fields as diverse as architecture, engineering, culinary arts, political science, and sustainability. Whether you are a future hotel manager, a chef-in-training, or a budding sustainability consultant, these guidelines will provide a multi-faceted understanding of what it takes to operate a green and socially responsible business.

It's important to note that the list of best practices outlined here is illustrative rather than comprehensive. The burgeoning field of sustainable hospitality is as dynamic as it is expansive, and the full list of lessons to be learned would be much, much larger. The goal here is to offer an overview that captures the essence of successful sustainable initiatives, providing a steppingstone for those committed to making a meaningful impact.

- **Emphasize Energy Efficiency, Water Conservation, and Waste Management**

Adopting advanced technologies and practices is non-negotiable for those in the hospitality industry aiming to minimize their environmental footprint. Investing in energy-efficient lighting, smart HVAC systems, and water-efficient fixtures, akin to what we observed in Hilton Hotels and NOMA, results in substantial reductions in both energy and water usage. Moreover, prioritizing waste management techniques not only curtails landfill contributions but also fosters a culture of responsible consumption.

- **Cultivate a Culture of Sustainability Among Staff and Guests**

Employee and guest engagement is pivotal to nurturing a sustainable ethos. Educational campaigns and interactive experiences, such as towel and linen reuse programs or in-room energy conservation tips, can encourage responsible behaviors. As seen in Marriott's Serve 360 program, a committed staff can act as sustainability ambassadors, catalyzing broader participation in eco-friendly practices among guests.

- **Build Partnerships with Local Suppliers**

Collaborating with local suppliers who share a commitment to sustainability not only shrinks the transportation-related carbon footprint but also bolsters local economies. As NOMA has exemplified with its local sourcing, strategic partnerships can facilitate a more holistic approach to sustainability that extends beyond the property's boundaries.

- **Prioritize Green Architecture and Design**

As architects and engineers are increasingly illustrating, sustainable construction and renovation techniques—like the use of sustainable materials, passive cooling, and integrated renewable energy systems—can greatly minimize environmental impact. This is vividly showcased by places like Chatham University's Eden Hall Campus, where green design is central to the institution's ethos.

- **Implement a Data-Driven Approach to Sustainability**

Adopting measurable sustainability metrics and seeking relevant certifications like LEED or Green Globe can serve as a roadmap for continuous improvement. Regular performance audits can help identify areas that require further innovation, thus demonstrating the establishment's commitment to sustainability to both customers and investors.

- **Adopt Circular Economy Principles**

Moving from a linear to a circular consumption model significantly elevates a hospitality business' sustainability efforts. Places like Seattle, with its ambitious Zero Waste Strategy, show that practices such as recycling, composting, and upcycling not only conserve resources but also reduce waste in a meaningful way.

- **Engage in Community and Social Stewardship**

Beyond environmental initiatives, true sustainability also involves social responsibility. Whether it's supporting local educational programs, contributing to charitable causes, or partnering on community projects, socially responsible practices can enhance a business's reputation and contribute positively to societal well-being.

These principles are not merely theoretical but are drawn from real-world success stories in the industry. They offer a comprehensive guide to those in the fields of hospitality, architecture, engineering, political science, and sustainability, showcasing the multi-disciplinary approach required to navigate the path to sustainability effectively.

## 11.3 Advancing Sustainable Hospitality: From Innovation to Implementation

In the quest for sustainability, embracing innovative technologies and systems is just one half of the equation. The other half involves strategic implementation—a stage where even the most groundbreaking technologies can stumble if not well-executed. This section delves into additional layers of complexity, exploring how successful green transformations in the hospitality sector go beyond initial adoption to create lasting change. Here, we will examine some of the pivotal considerations that enable a smooth transition from conventional to green operations.

One of the foremost considerations is developing a robust sustainability plan, a roadmap that sets forth clear objectives, actionable tasks, and measurable outcomes. It's not enough to implement eco-friendly practices sporadically; there must be a structured approach that takes into account various aspects, from energy and water usage to waste management. Using interdisciplinary insights from architects, engineers, and political scientists, this plan should encompass the overall layout and design of the property, energy systems, and operational logistics, such as sourcing of food items and waste handling.

## Building a Multidisciplinary Team

A holistic approach to sustainability often involves forming a multidisciplinary team of experts who can address the multi-faceted challenges that come with transitioning to greener operations. For example, chefs can bring a unique perspective on sourcing local and sustainable food, reducing waste in the kitchen, and using energy-efficient cooking methods. Engineers can guide the installation and maintenance of state-of-the-art green technologies, such as advanced HVAC systems, solar panels, or water-saving fixtures. The inclusion of experts in political science can also provide a nuanced understanding of local and international regulatory frameworks that govern sustainability practices.

This team not only helps in the initial planning and implementation phases but also plays a vital role in the ongoing monitoring and optimization of green initiatives. It's an evolving process, one that requires continuous adaptation to new technologies, best practices, and regulatory changes. This underscores the importance of making sustainability an integral part of the organizational culture. For example, Scandic Hotels involves all levels of employees, from management to housekeeping, in their sustainability journey. Similarly, Microsoft's Global Headquarters in Redmond, Washington, leverages a cross-disciplinary team to manage its extensive green initiatives, ranging from building design to daily operations.

## Scaling Green Practices Across the Business

While it is essential to start with focused, manageable initiatives, the ultimate goal is to scale these across the entire business. Taking a leaf from Google's Bayview Campus, where an all-electric approach is woven into the very fabric of the campus design, it's important to build scalability into the initial plan. This ensures that successful pilot projects can be rolled out more broadly, optimizing the impact of sustainable practices on the establishment's overall carbon footprint.

Scalability also includes taking successful implementations from one property and replicating them across other properties in a chain. Hilton, for example, has been able to roll out its energy-efficient technologies across multiple hotels, thereby amplifying the environmental benefits. Furthermore, scalability isn't just about breadth but also depth. As seen in the case of Chatham University's Eden Hall Campus, which serves as a model for sustainability in higher education, adopting a range of complementary green initiatives can create a ripple effect, reinforcing each other to create a more robust and comprehensive sustainability program.

## Leveraging Technology for Continuous Improvement

Technology plays a pivotal role in the journey towards sustainability. The integration of smart systems for energy management, water conservation, and waste reduction not only allows for real-time monitoring but also for predictive analytics. Advanced analytics can identify patterns and trends, helping businesses preemptively address issues before they escalate.

However, technology is not a set-and-forget solution. It's vital to stay updated on the latest advancements in green technology to continually optimize performance. For instance, NOMA in Copenhagen used cutting-edge kitchen appliances that not only met but exceeded their current energy efficiency standards. As technology evolves, the restaurant was committed to updating its appliances, thereby perpetuating its cycle of continuous improvement.

By taking these additional dimensions into account, the roadmap to sustainability becomes more nuanced but also more effective. Transitioning to green operations is indeed complex, but with thoughtful planning, interdisciplinary expertise, and a commitment to continuous improvement, it is not just possible but profitable and rewarding.

## Conclusion

As we've explored in this chapter, the transition to sustainable practices within the hospitality industry is not merely a trendy option but an imperative for the long-term success and environmental responsibility of any establishment. Through various case studies and practical examples, ranging from giants like Hilton and Marriott to culinary leaders like NOMA, we've seen that achieving sustainability is complex but entirely feasible. Whether it's through energy-efficient design, local sourcing, waste management, or employee engagement, multiple pathways exist to drastically reduce an establishment's carbon footprint and make a meaningful contribution to the green industrial revolution.

However, it's important to remember that the examples and lessons outlined here are merely a snapshot of the myriad possibilities that exist. As technology advances and more businesses join the sustainability train, new methods and best practices will emerge. The challenge is to remain flexible, adaptable, and committed to learning and improving. By doing so, the hospitality industry can play a significant role in shaping a more sustainable and equitable future, setting standards, and offering lessons that can be applied across other sectors as well.

# CHAPTER 12

# FUTURE TRENDS AND OPPORTUNITIES IN THE GREEN INDUSTRIAL REVOLUTION

The world is standing at the precipice of a transformative era—the Green Industrial Revolution. This revolution is not just a response to the growing environmental challenges that threaten our planet but also an unprecedented opportunity to reshape industries, economies, and societies. As we confront the pressing need to reduce carbon emissions, conserve resources, and transition towards sustainable practices, we find ourselves on the cusp of a new wave of innovation and change. In this exploration, we delve into the future trends and opportunities that the Green Industrial Revolution promises, offering a glimpse into how emerging technologies, policies, and global shifts are poised to reshape our world in profound ways.

## 12.1 Emerging trends and technologies in the green industrial revolution

As we sail deeper into the 21st century, the green industrial revolution is accelerating, making indelible marks on industries across the board, particularly in the hospitality sector. The unfolding landscape is one of constant innovation, driven by a confluence of disciplines including architecture, engineering, culinary arts, political science, and sustainability. The green revolution is not only an imperative for planetary health but also offers compelling new opportunities for businesses ready to embrace change.

**Renewable Energy and Advanced Storage**

One of the foremost trends powering this revolution is the transition to renewable energy sources like solar and wind power. Unlike the traditional fossil fuel-dependent systems that have been the industry standard, renewable sources offer cleaner, more sustainable options. As solar panels and wind turbines become more affordable, it's becoming increasingly viable for hotels and resorts to install these systems. Coupled with advancements in energy storage, such as high-capacity batteries, businesses now have the tools to ensure energy stability even when renewable sources are inconsistent. In essence, the architecture and engineering of energy systems are going through a radical shift, promising more sustainable operations.

**Smart Grid Systems**

The advent of smart grids, which leverage cutting-edge communication and monitoring technologies, is another transformative development. These systems enable real-time monitoring and control of electricity distribution, optimizing energy flow and reliability. For the hospitality industry, this means greater efficiency in managing the energy demands of large establishments that can vary considerably with fluctuating occupancy rates. Engineers and IT professionals are collaborating to create these highly integrated systems, leading to more dynamic energy management and reduced wastage.

## Electrification of Transportation

The rapid rise of electric vehicles (EVs) is a game-changer for both the transportation and hospitality sectors. With expanding charging infrastructure, hotels, and resorts have the opportunity to facilitate this transition by installing charging stations, thereby encouraging sustainable travel options for guests and employees. This approach synergizes with local and national efforts to reduce greenhouse gas emissions, showcasing how the hospitality sector can actively participate in the larger sustainability agenda.

## Green Building Practices

The integration of green building practices into architectural designs marks a significant shift toward sustainability. These practices incorporate elements like LED lights, energy-efficient insulation, and passive cooling to minimize energy consumption. Sourcing materials locally and ensuring they are recycled, or recyclable adds another layer to the sustainability matrix. This holistic approach to construction and design underscores how architects and sustainability experts can collaborate to make strides in reducing the hospitality industry's carbon footprint.

## Circular Economy and Waste Management

Adoption of circular economy principles is a rising trend. By recycling, reusing, and refurbishing products, businesses can conserve resources and significantly reduce waste. Composting and waste-to-energy technologies can also be incorporated into the waste management strategies of hotels and restaurants, particularly in the kitchen areas which are substantial contributors to the carbon footprint. Chefs and sustainability officers are increasingly joining forces to make these principles a lived reality.

## AI and Data-Driven Sustainability

Finally, the integration of artificial intelligence (AI) and data analytics is heralding a transformative phase in intelligent sustainability management. These sophisticated technologies have the capability to forecast energy consumption patterns, dynamically adjust operational systems, and pinpoint opportunities for energy conservation. The convergence of technology and sustainability has enabled a new paradigm of data-driven decision-making, which has profound implications for reducing an establishment's carbon footprint and enhancing its operational efficiency. In innovative applications, AI is beginning to extend its reach into the culinary realm, showing potential in optimizing cooking processes by precisely regulating oven temperatures based on the quantity and mass of what is inside, for instance.

In summary, the green industrial revolution is a kaleidoscope of emerging technologies and strategies that are redefining what is possible in terms of environmental stewardship and operational efficiency. As these trends continue to evolve, they offer a plethora of opportunities for the hospitality industry to reduce carbon footprints, enhance efficiency, and meet the ever-growing demands of eco-conscious consumers. By staying ahead of these developments, the hospitality sector is well-positioned to contribute significantly to a more sustainable global economy.

## 12.2 Potential Challenges and Opportunities in the Future of the Hospitality Industry

The trajectory of the hospitality industry is irrevocably linked to the ongoing quest for sustainable and ethical practices. As global consciousness around environmental issues amplifies, travelers are progressively opting for accommodations that resonate with their eco-conscious ethos. This paradigm shift in consumer behavior presents a complex web of challenges and opportunities for the hospitality sector. The ensuing sections aim to dissect these challenges and opportunities, setting the stage for how the hospitality industry can navigate a path toward a future that is both sustainable and attuned to evolving guest preferences.

Challenges:

*1. Adapting to Dynamic Consumer Preferences:*

The fluid nature of eco-conscious consumer expectations necessitates agility and adaptability within the hospitality industry. Keeping pace with guest demands for cutting-edge green technologies and sustainable amenities challenges businesses to be innovative, nimble, and proactive in adopting eco-friendly practices. This active responsiveness not only fortifies a business's market standing but also engenders a dedicated following among environmentally aware travelers.

## 2. Navigating Regulatory Landscapes:

Global and national policy landscapes are increasingly prioritizing environmental sustainability, manifesting in more stringent regulatory requirements for hospitality businesses. Navigating these evolving regulations demands continuous oversight and significant investments in eco-friendly technologies and practices. Compliance not only aids in averting legal repercussions but also serves to affirm a business's commitment to sustainability, fortifying its credibility and trust among stakeholders.

## 3. Managing Initial Operational Expenses:

Initial financial outlays for sustainable technologies and practices can be a stumbling block for some establishments in the hospitality sector. Investments in facility upgrades, advanced technologies, and staff education might temporarily inflate operational costs. However, such expenditures frequently translate into long-term cost efficiencies as resource-conserving practices bring down utility and waste management expenses.

## 4. Addressing Talent Gaps:

Securing a workforce that is both skilled and passionate about sustainability is a formidable challenge for the hospitality industry. Investment in robust training programs and offering incentives for participation in sustainability initiatives can ameliorate this issue. A well-informed and motivated workforce becomes an asset in implementing green strategies, which not only enriches the guest experience but also augments an establishment's repute as a sustainable destination.

Opportunities:

*1. Strategic Differentiation:*

Commitment to sustainability offers a distinctive edge in a competitive marketplace. By adopting and showcasing green practices, like waste-to-energy technologies or AI-driven energy management, hospitality businesses can appeal to a burgeoning cohort of eco-aware guests.

*2. Capitalizing on the Eco-conscious Traveler:*

The burgeoning trend of eco-conscious travel spells a burgeoning market for sustainable hospitality solutions. These travelers are not just consumers; they are allies in environmental stewardship who are actively seeking out hotels and resorts that share their sustainable values.

*3. Cost-Efficiency Through Sustainability:*

Green practices—ranging from simple measures like energy-efficient lighting to more complex initiatives like smart grids—ultimately contribute to operational cost reductions. These savings in utility bills and waste management can improve the financial performance of a business over time.

*4. Technological Leverage for Personalized Experiences:*

Emerging technologies offer a double boon—enhanced guest experiences and sustainability. Think smart rooms that adjust lighting and temperature based on occupancy, or AI systems that optimize resource use without compromising guest comfort.

*5. Community Collaboration for Mutual Benefit:*

Engagement with local communities can offer a twofold advantage: It can provide guests with authentic experiences while also preserving local ecosystems and cultures. Working in tandem with local suppliers and artisans not only fosters good community relationships but also contributes to local economic and sustainable development.

In charting their course toward a sustainable future, the hospitality industry faces a blend of challenges and opportunities. Through the strategic adoption of green practices and technologies, the sector can not only enhance its environmental stewardship but also attract a new generation of eco-conscious travelers. In doing so, it takes steps toward shaping a more sustainable and guest-centric future, thereby contributing positively to both industry innovation and global sustainability efforts.

## 12.3 Building a Holistic Sustainable Model: Interdisciplinary Approaches & Stakeholder Involvement

As we delve deeper into the intertwining strands of sustainability and hospitality, it becomes increasingly clear that addressing the challenges and seizing the opportunities is not a unilateral effort. A multidisciplinary approach, integrating insights from architecture, engineering, culinary arts, political science, and sustainability studies, is essential for building a comprehensive sustainable model in the hospitality industry. Let's explore how these interdisciplinary perspectives can enrich and inform sustainable practices, and why stakeholder involvement is crucial for success.

## Interdisciplinary Approaches:

*1. Architectural Innovations:*

Sustainable architectural practices have the potential to significantly reduce the carbon footprint of hospitality establishments. Passive design strategies, such as natural lighting and cooling, can drastically cut down energy consumption. The architectural concept extends beyond just the building to the landscape, optimizing natural resources and providing a holistic experience for guests.

*2. Engineering Solutions:*

Engineers can devise efficient systems for waste management, water purification, and renewable energy usage. Technologies like advanced HVAC systems can be integrated into building designs to create an environmentally sound and cost-efficient infrastructure.

*3. Culinary Sustainability:*

Chefs and culinary experts bring a unique perspective to sustainability by focusing on sourcing local produce, minimizing food waste, and optimizing kitchen practices. By employing sustainable cooking technologies, chefs can create delightful dishes that are not just palate-pleasers but also planet-friendly.

*4. Political Science and Policy Alignment:*

Understanding the political landscape and the shifting sands of regulations and incentives can give hospitality businesses a competitive edge. Political scientists can help in interpreting how global, national, and local policies might affect sustainability initiatives, allowing businesses to anticipate challenges and adapt strategies accordingly.

*5. Sustainability Science:*

Expertise in sustainability can provide the theoretical and practical foundation for implementing green practices. From conducting life cycle assessments for products to creating sustainability reports, these experts can offer tools to measure and enhance environmental performance.

**Stakeholder Involvement:**

*1. Guests as Partners:*

Hospitality businesses can foster a sense of community and shared responsibility by involving guests in sustainability initiatives. From offering incentives for reusing towels to educating them on local environmental challenges, guest involvement makes the journey toward sustainability a collaborative effort.

*2. Employee Engagement:*

Employees are the backbone of sustainability efforts in any organization. Through ongoing training and inclusion in decision-making processes, staff members can be turned into sustainability champions who enact and promote green practices on a daily basis.

*3. Local Community and Suppliers:*

A synergistic relationship with the local community and suppliers can serve to enhance the sustainability quotient. Whether it's sourcing locally grown organic food or collaborating with local artisans for decor, the involvement of community stakeholders can create a ripple effect of sustainability.

*4. Investors and Shareholders:*

Financial stakeholders can be the catalysts in driving sustainability initiatives. By recognizing the long-term benefits of a green approach, they are more likely to invest in sustainable technologies and practices, giving the business the financial leverage, it needs to go green.

As the hospitality sector journeys toward a sustainable future, the integration of multidisciplinary insights and broad stakeholder involvement becomes not just advantageous but essential. By fostering a culture of collaboration and inclusivity, the industry is better equipped to meet the evolving challenges of sustainability while offering guests an experience that is both luxurious and responsible. This holistic approach ensures that sustainability in the hospitality industry becomes a shared goal, where various disciplines and stakeholders come together to effect meaningful change.

# APPENDIX: ADDITIONAL RESOURCES & TERMINOLOGY

In this Appendix, we offer supplemental materials and explanations for key terms and concepts introduced in this book. These resources are aimed at enhancing your understanding of the initial framework for the green industrial revolution as it relates to the hospitality industry and are broken up by chapter.

## Chapter 1

**Glossary of Key Terms:**

1. **Sustainability**- The practice of meeting the needs of the present without compromising the ability of future generations to meet their own needs.

2. **Renewable Energy**- Energy produced from sources that do not deplete or can be replenished within a human's lifetime.

3. **Carbon Footprint**- The total amount of greenhouse gases produced, directly and indirectly, by human activities.

4. **Green Industrial Revolution**- A transformative movement that integrates sustainable, renewable energy and technologies into the fabric of existing economic and social systems, aiming to reduce greenhouse gas emissions and dependency on fossil fuels.

5. **Hospitality Sector**- The broad category of fields within the service industry that include lodging, food and drink service, event planning, and tourism.

6. **Smart Grids**- Electric grid systems that use digital technology to better manage and distribute energy.

7. **Electrification**- The process of replacing other forms of energy with electrical energy.

8. **Circular Economy-** An economic system aimed at eliminating waste and the continual use of resources.

## Online Resources

1. U.S. Environmental Protection Agency (EPA) - Provides extensive resources on sustainable practices and regulations.

   - Website: https://www.epa.gov/

2. World Green Building Council- Offers insights into sustainable architecture and building practices.

   - Website: https://www.worldgbc.org/

3. Clean Energy Council- Comprehensive resource for renewable energy technologies and policy advice.

   - Website: https://www.cleanenergycouncil.org.au/

4. Green Hotelier- Focused on best practices in sustainability within the hospitality industry.

   - Website: https://www.greenhotelier.org/

5. International Renewable Energy Agency (IRENA)- Resource center for global renewable energy data.

   - Website: https://www.irena.org/

## Recommended Readings

1. "Sustainable Hospitality: Eco-Friendly Practices for the Hotel Industry" by Richard J. Cohen

   - A comprehensive guide on implementing sustainable practices in the hospitality industry.

2. "The Green Industrial Revolution: Energy, Engineering and Economics" by Woodrow W. Clark II and Grant Cooke

   - A critical look at the rise of green technologies and their economic impact.

3. "Clean Disruption of Energy and Transportation" by Tony Seba

   - Focuses on how renewable energy and electric vehicles are transforming industries.

4. "EcoMind: Changing the Way We Think, to Create the World We Want" by Frances Moore Lappé

   - Explores how mindset influences our relationship with sustainability.

5. "Thinking in Systems: A Primer" by Donella H. Meadows

   - An introduction to systems thinking, relevant for understanding the complex networks of sustainability.

## Studies

1. "The Role of Renewable Energy in the Hospitality Industry: An Analysis"

   - Focuses on the practical application of renewable energy sources in hotels and resorts.

2. "Consumer Attitudes Toward Sustainable Hospitality"

   - Explores how consumer preferences are shifting towards eco-friendly hospitality services.

3. "Green Building Technologies: Implications for the Hospitality Industry"

   - An in-depth study on the impact of green architecture and building practices in the hospitality sector.

4. "Political Policies and their Influence on Sustainable Practices in Hospitality"

   - Looks at how governmental policies at various levels affect the implementation of green practices in the hospitality industry.

5. "Smart Grid Applications in Sustainable Hospitality"

   - Studies the role of smart grids in optimizing energy consumption in hotels and resorts.

# Chapter 2

Glossary of Key Terms:

1. **Energy Efficiency**- The practice of reducing energy consumption while maintaining the same output level, thus doing more with less energy.

2. **Traditional Gas Counterparts**- Conventional gas-powered systems or machinery that can be replaced with more efficient or green alternatives.

3. **Health Impact**- The effect of a particular activity or substance on human health, either positive or negative.

4. **Economic Viability**- The feasibility of a project or practice in terms of its potential for long-term financial sustainability.

5. **Climate Impact**- The effect of an activity, substance, or policy on global or local climate conditions.

6. **Innovation Adoption**- The process by which new technologies or practices are accepted and implemented by individuals or organizations.

7. **Low-Carbon Technologies**- Technologies designed to produce energy or perform tasks with minimal greenhouse gas emissions.

## Online Resources

1. International Energy Agency (IEA)- Provides data, reports, and guides about global energy trends including energy efficiency.

   - Website: https://www.iea.org/

2. Green Tech Media- Source for green technology news, including innovations in energy efficiency.

   - Website: https://www.greentechmedia.com/

3. American Council for an Energy-Efficient Economy (ACEEE) - Provides information on policies and practices for energy efficiency.

   - Website: https://www.aceee.org/

4. Health and Environment Alliance- Focuses on the link between health impacts and environmental policy.

   - Website: https://www.env-health.org/

5. The Carbon Trust- Provides sustainability certification and consultancy services, focusing on reducing carbon emissions.

   - Website: https://www.carbontrust.com/

## Recommended Readings

1. "The Future of Energy: Earth, Wind and Fire" by Amanda Little

   - Discusses innovations in energy technology and their potential impact on the future.

2. "Hot, Flat, and Crowded" by Thomas Friedman

   - Discusses the need for a green revolution in the context of climate change and globalization.

3. "Sustainable Energy – Without the Hot Air" by David JC MacKay

- A practical guide to understanding energy efficiency and renewable energy options.

4. "The Health Effects of Climate Change" by Jonathan A. Patz

   - Discusses the connections between climate change and public health.

5. "The Circular Economy Handbook" by Peter Lacy and Jessica Long

   - Explains the principles and benefits of the circular economy, particularly relevant for industries looking to adopt low-carbon technologies.

6. "The Building Decarbonization Practice Guide" – The William J. Worthen Foundation

- Offers a comprehensive understanding of the implications of building decarbonization. Serves as a practical resource for professionals in construction & hospitality sectors aiming to adopt sustainable building practices.

## Studies

1. "Adoption Barriers for Low-Carbon Technologies in the Hospitality Industry"

   - Investigates the factors that prevent the adoption of low-carbon technologies in the hospitality sector.

2. "Energy Efficiency in Hotels: A Cost-Benefit Analysis"

- Compares the costs and benefits of implementing energy-efficient technologies in hotels.

3. "Health Impacts of Climate-Smart Choices in the Hospitality Industry"

  - Evaluates how green technologies can improve both environmental and public health outcomes.

4. "The Economic Viability of Green Practices in Hospitality"

  - Examines the financial implications of adopting green technologies and practices in the hospitality industry.

5. "Assessing the Climate Impact of the Hospitality Sector"

  - Uses data to quantify the effect of the hospitality sector on climate change and suggests potential mitigating strategies.

# Chapter 3

## Glossary of Key Terms

1. **Sustainable Development**: Development that meets the needs of the present without compromising the ability of future generations to meet their own needs.

2. **Carbon Footprint**: The total amount of greenhouse gases that are emitted into the atmosphere as a result of human activities.

3. **Renewable Energy**: Energy generated from natural resources such as sunlight, wind, and water, which are renewable (naturally replenished).

4. **Green Hospitality**: The practice of hotels and other establishments in the hospitality industry adopting sustainable operations and eco-friendly technologies.

5. **Sustainability Metrics**: Tools or indicators used to measure the environmental, social, and economic impacts of a particular action or policy.

6. **Waste-to-Energy Technologies**: Technologies that generate energy in the form of electricity or heat from the primary treatment of waste.

7. **Hospitality Sector:** A broad category of fields within the service industry that includes lodging, food and drink service, event planning, and travel and tourism.

## Online Resources

1. Global Reporting Initiative (GRI): Provides standards for sustainability reporting.

   - Website: https://www.globalreporting.org/

2. Green Seal: A non-profit organization that uses science-based programs to empower consumers, purchasers, and companies to create a more sustainable world.

   - Website: https://www.greenseal.org/

3. World Green Building Council: A network of national green building councils in more than one hundred countries, which aims to make all buildings more sustainable.

   - Website: https://www.worldgbc.org/

4. EPA's Sustainable Practices: Resources and guidelines for sustainable management policies.

   - Website: https://www.epa.gov/sustainability

5. The International Ecotourism Society (TIES): Provides resources and guidelines for making travel and tourism more sustainable.

   - Website: https://www.ecotourism.org/

## Recommended Readings

1. "The Green Imperative" by Victor Papanek

   - Discusses the environmental responsibilities of designers and businesses, relevant for sustainable development in the hospitality sector.

2. "Cradle to Cradle: Remaking the Way We Make Things" by William McDonough & Michael Braungart

   - Focuses on the lifecycle of products and materials, particularly useful for understanding waste-to-energy technologies.

3. "The New Rules of Green Marketing" by Jacquelyn Ottman

   - Examines how businesses can benefit from adopting green and sustainable practices.

4. "Sustainable Hospitality: Eco-friendly Practices in Hotels and other Hospitality and Tourist Facilities" by Sonya Graci and Jackie Kuehnel

   - Focuses specifically on the hospitality sector, outlining best practices and case studies.

5. "Tourism and Sustainability: Development, Globalisation and New Tourism in the Third World" by Martin Mowforth and Ian Munt

   - Discusses the complexities of making the global tourism industry more sustainable.

6. "The Building Decarbonization Practice Guide" – The William J. Worthen Foundation

- Offers a comprehensive understanding of the implications of building decarbonization. Serves as a practical resource for professionals in construction & hospitality sectors aiming to adopt sustainable building practices.

## Studies

1. "Impact of Sustainable Practices on Guest Satisfaction and Loyalty"

   - Explores the link between sustainable practices in the hospitality sector and guest satisfaction and loyalty.

2. "Carbon Footprinting in the Hospitality Industry"

   - Provides an analysis of carbon footprints in various types of hospitality establishments.

3. "Economic Feasibility of Renewable Energy in Three-Star Hotels"

   - Investigates the economic implications of adopting renewable energy sources in mid-level hotels.

4. "Measuring Sustainability in the Hospitality Industry"

- Outlines different metrics and tools to measure sustainability in the hospitality industry.

5. "Behavioral Study of Waste-to-Energy Adoption in Five-Star Hotels"

   - Explores behavioral factors affecting the adoption of waste-to-energy technologies in luxury hotels.

# Chapter 4

## Glossary of Key Terms

1. **Energy Efficiency**: The goal to reduce the amount of energy required to provide products and services.

2. **Carbon Neutral**: Achieving net-zero carbon dioxide emissions by balancing carbon emissions with carbon removal or offsetting.

3. **Circular Economy**: An economic system aimed at eliminating waste and promoting the continual use of resources

4. **Life Cycle Assessment (LCA)**: The assessment of the environmental impacts of a product or service throughout its entire life cycle.

5. **Local Sourcing**: The practice of purchasing products or services that are locally produced to reduce carbon footprint due to transportation.

6. **Organic Produce**: Foods that are grown without the use of synthetic pesticides, bioengineered genes, or petroleum-based fertilizers.

7. **Composting**: The process of recycling decomposed organic material into rich soil.

8. **LED Lights**: Light-emitting diode lights that are more energy-efficient than traditional incandescent bulbs.

## Online Resources

1. ENERGY STAR for Hospitality: Provides guidelines for energy-efficient appliances and building practices.

   - Website: https://www.energystar.gov/buildings

2. Green Key: An eco-label awarded to sustainable businesses in the tourism industry.

   - Website: https://www.greenkey.global/

3. Local Harvest: Connects people looking for good food with the farmers who produce it.

   - Website: https://www.localharvest.org/

4. Zero Waste Alliance: Provides resources for achieving zero waste and circular economy goals.

   - Website: http://www.zerowaste.org/

5. Sustainable Food Lab: Facilitates market-based solutions to food sustainability.

   - Website: https://sustainablefoodlab.org/

## Recommended Readings

1. "Drawdown: The Most Comprehensive Plan Ever Proposed to Reverse Global Warming" by Paul Hawken

   - Provides a detailed plan addressing various sectors, including hospitality, to reverse global warming.

2. "Green to Gold" by Daniel C. Esty and Andrew S. Winston

   - Discusses how companies can profit from environmental awareness.

3. "The Omnivore's Dilemma" by Michael Pollan

   - Explores the ethical and environmental implications of eating, applicable to food sourcing in hospitality.

4. "Waste to Wealth: The Circular Economy Advantage" by Peter Lacy & Jakob Rutqvist

   - Highlights the economic advantages of adopting a circular economy model.

5. "Hospitality 2050: The Future of Hospitality and Travel" by Ian Yeoman and Una McMahon-Beattie

   - Offers futuristic scenarios for the hospitality industry, including environmental considerations.

6. "The Building Decarbonization Practice Guide" – The William J. Worthen Foundation

- Offers a comprehensive understanding of the implications of building decarbonization. Serves as a practical resource for professionals in construction & hospitality sectors aiming to adopt sustainable building practices.

## Studies

1. "The Efficacy of LED Lighting in the Hospitality Industry"

   - Investigates the cost-saving and environmental benefits of switching to LED lighting in hotels and restaurants.

2. "Carbon Neutrality and the Hospitality Sector"

   - Examines the feasibility of achieving carbon neutrality within the hospitality sector.

3. "Sustainable Sourcing in the Hotel Industry"

   - Analyzes the benefits and challenges of local and sustainable sourcing in hotels.

4. "Consumer Perceptions of Food Waste Reduction Initiatives"

   - Discusses how food waste reduction impacts consumer choice and perception in the hospitality industry.

5. "Economic Analysis of Composting in the Hospitality Sector"

   - Evaluates the economic benefits of composting food waste in hotels and restaurants.

# Chapter 5

Glossary of Key Terms:

1. **Sustainable Tourism**: Tourism that takes full account of its current and future economic, social, and environmental impacts, addressing the needs of visitors, the industry, the environment, and host communities.

2. **Green Certification**: A form of environmental regulation and sustainable design certification that empowers professionals and organizations to take ownership of their projects.

3. **Water Conservation**: Any beneficial reduction of water usage, loss, or waste.

4. **Recycling**: The action or process of converting waste into reusable material.

5. **Eco-Friendly Amenities**: Products and services designed to do the least possible damage to the environment.

6. **Local Partnerships**: Collaborations with local businesses and organizations to enhance sustainability and benefit the community.

7. **Supply Chain Management**: The management of the flow of goods and services, involves the movement and storage of raw materials, of work-in-process inventory, and of finished goods from point of origin to point of consumption.

8. **Corporate Social Responsibility (CSR)**: A business model that helps a company be socially accountable to itself, its stakeholders, and the public.

## Online Resources

1. TripAdvisor's Green Leaders Program: Helps travelers make greener choices by recognizing hotels engaging in environmentally friendly practices.

   - Website: https://www.tripadvisor.com/GreenLeaders

2. Green Seal: Provides science-based environmental certification standards that are credible, transparent, and essential in an increasingly educated and competitive marketplace.

   - Website: https://greenseal.org/

3. Fair Trade Certified: Helps you to find companies committed to sustainability so that you can shop and travel with confidence.

   - Website: https://www.fairtradecertified.org/

4. LEED (Leadership in Energy and Environmental Design): Provides a framework for healthy, highly efficient, and cost-saving green buildings.

   - Website: https://www.usgbc.org/leed

5. WELL Building Standard: Focuses on advancing health and well-being in buildings and communities.

   - Website: https://www.wellcertified.com/

6. EPA (Environmental Protection Agency): Offers guidelines, regulations, and resources on various environmental issues, including waste management and air quality.

   - Website: https://www.epa.gov/

7. WaterSense: WaterSense, an EPA program, promotes water efficiency by certifying water-saving products and encouraging water-conservation practices in the hospitality industry.

- Website: https://www.epa.gov/watersense

8. Safer Choice: Safer Choice, an EPA initiative, advocates for safer chemical products, encouraging the use of environmentally friendly cleaning solutions in hotels and resorts.

Website: https://www.epa.gov/saferchoice

9. Sustainable Purchasing: EPA's Sustainable Purchasing program provides guidelines for environmentally preferable product procurement, guiding the hospitality industry toward sustainable sourcing practices.

- Website: https://www.epa.gov/greenerproducts

10. Sustainable Management of Food: Focused on reducing food waste, the EPA's Sustainable Management of Food program promotes strategies for hotels and restaurants to minimize waste and enhance sustainability in their food operations. Website: https://www.epa.gov/sustainable-management-food

11. BREEMA (Building Research Establishment Environmental Assessment Method): Provides certification for sustainable building and construction practices.

   - Website: https://www.breeam.com/

12. ILFI (International Living Future Institute): Provides a variety of certification programs and resources that promote sustainability and ecological stewardship.

- Website: https://living-future.org/

13. Forward Dining Solutions: National experts innovating and empowering hospitality businesses with sustainable strategies for waste reduction, energy efficiency, and ethical design.

- Website: https://www.ForwardDiningSolutions.com

14. EcoChef: Created by industry leading experts championing eco-friendly practices by standardizing how kitchens are designed, built, and operated.

- Website www.ecochef.org

These additional resources further enrich the available information on sustainability, building practices, and environmental responsibility, supplementing the content discussed in Chapter 5.

## Recommended Readings

1. "Sustainable Hospitality and Tourism as Motors for Development" by Paulina Bohdanowicz and Rachel Dodds

   - Explores case studies highlighting the role of tourism in sustainable development.

2. "Green Teams: Engaging Employees in Sustainability" by Matthew W. Tueth

   - Discusses the importance of employee engagement in sustainable initiatives.

3. "Overbooked: The Exploding Business of Travel and Tourism" by Elizabeth Becker

- A deep dive into the tourism industry, examining its impact on the environment and how it can be made more sustainable.

4. "Let My People Go Surfing" by Yvon Chouinard

   - The philosophy of Patagonia's founder, useful for hospitality leaders looking to inject sustainability into their corporate culture.

5. "Tourism and Water" by Stefan Gössling, C. Michael Hall, and Daniel Scott

   - This book explores the complicated relationship between tourism and water resources management.

6. "The Building Decarbonization Practice Guide" – The William J. Worthen Foundation

- Offers a comprehensive understanding of the implications of building decarbonization. Serves as a practical resource for professionals in construction & hospitality sectors aiming to adopt sustainable building practices.

## Studies

1. "The Impact of Green Certification on Hotel Guest Satisfaction"

   - Investigates whether green certification actually correlates with higher levels of guest satisfaction.

2. "Sustainability in the Hotel Industry: An Examination of the Application of the Triple Bottom Line"

   - Evaluates the Triple Bottom Line framework as it applies to the sustainability practices of hotels.

3. "Corporate Social Responsibility in the Hospitality Sector"

   - A study focusing on how CSR initiatives affect employee morale, customer satisfaction, and overall profitability.

4. "The Feasibility of Water-Saving Technologies in Hotels"

   - An evaluation of technologies like low-flow faucets and their economic and environmental impact.

5. "Local Sourcing in the Hospitality Industry: Benefits and Challenges"

   - Explores the advantages and limitations of sourcing locally in terms of cost, supply chain logistics, and sustainability impact.

# Chapter 6

## Glossary of Key Terms

1. **Carbon Footprint**: The total amount of greenhouse gases produced to directly and indirectly support human activities, usually expressed in equivalent tons of carbon dioxide (CO2e).

2. **Renewable Energy**: Energy from a source that is not depleted when used, such as wind or solar power.

3. **Energy Efficiency**: The goal to reduce the amount of energy required to provide products and services.

4. **Zero-Waste Philosophy**: An approach to resources and waste management that mimics sustainable natural cycles, aiming to eliminate the volume and toxicity of waste and materials.

5. **Food Waste Management**: Practices to minimize food wastage through reduction, recovery, and recycling techniques.

6. **LEED Certification**: A globally recognized symbol of sustainability achievement and leadership.

7. **IoT (Internet of Things):** A system of interrelated computing devices, mechanical and digital machines, objects, animals, or people provided with unique identifiers (UIDs) and the ability to transfer data over a network without requiring human-to-human or human-to-computer interaction.

8. **Greenwashing**: The practice of making an unsubstantiated or misleading claim about the environmental benefits of a product, service, or technology.

## Online Resources

1. US Green Building Council: Provides LEED certification guidelines and resources.

   - Website: https://www.usgbc.org/

2. ENERGY STAR for Hotels: Offers advice and resources for improving energy efficiency in hotels.

   - Website: https://www.energystar.gov/

3. Waste Management's Sustainability Services: Offers a comprehensive approach to reducing waste and improving sustainability.

   - Website: https://www.wm.com/us/en/business/sustainability-services

## Recommended Readings

1. "The New Rules of Green Marketing" by Jacquelyn Ottman

   - Strategies, tools, and inspiration for sustainable branding.

2. "Cradle to Cradle: Remaking the Way We Make Things" by William McDonough & Michael Braungart

   - A manifesto calling for a new industrial revolution, one that would render both traditional manufacturing and traditional environmentalism obsolete.

3. "Zero Waste Home" by Bea Johnson

   - A guide to simplifying your life by reducing waste.

4. "The Circular Economy Handbook" by Peter Lacy, Jessica Long, and Wesley Spindler

   - An actionable guide for business leaders in adaptation and implementation of circular economy concepts.

5. "Sustainable Energy – Without the Hot Air" by David J.C. MacKay

   - A straightforward evaluation of the most sustainable energy options available.

6. "The Building Decarbonization Practice Guide" – The William J. Worthen Foundation

- Offers a comprehensive understanding of the implications of building decarbonization. Serves as a practical resource for professionals in construction & hospitality sectors aiming to adopt sustainable building practices.

## Studies

1. "Energy Efficiency and Conservation in Hotels – Towards Sustainable Tourism"

   - Analyzes how different types of hotels are adopting energy-efficient practices.

2. "The Role of Renewable Energy in the Hotel Sector: An Analysis"

   - A study on the adoption and efficiency of renewable energy sources in hotels.

3. "Understanding Food Waste in the Hospitality Sector"

   - Quantitative and qualitative insights into food waste management in hotels.

4. "Greenwashing in the Hospitality Industry"

   - Investigates the incidence and impact of misleading environmental claims in the hotel industry.

5. "The Impact of IoT in Hospitality: An Overview"

   - Evaluates the role and impact of IoT technologies in enhancing energy efficiency and guest experience in the hotel sector.

# Chapter 7

## Glossary of Key Terms

1. **Sustainable Procurement**: The process of purchasing goods and services that take into account the social, economic, and environmental impact.

2. **Locavore Movement**: A trend where consumers prefer to eat locally-sourced and produced food to minimize carbon footprint.

3. **Green Supply Chain**: A sustainable supply chain that involves the production and distribution of goods in a manner that minimizes environmental and social risks.

4. **Organic Foods**: Foods produced without the use of synthetic fertilizers, pesticides, or genetically modified organisms.

5. **Farm-to-Table**: A food system in which food is produced locally and delivered to local consumers.

6. **CSR (Corporate Social Responsibility)**: A business model that helps a company be socially accountable to itself, its stakeholders, and the public.

7. **Eco-labeling**: A labeling system for consumer products that indicates a product's environmental impact.

8. **Lifecycle Analysis**: The assessment of the environmental impacts of a product or service throughout its lifecycle.

## Online Resources

1. Sustainable Food Trade Association: Provides tools and resources to help food companies adopt sustainable practices.

   - Website: https://www.sustainablefoodtrade.org/

2. Green Seal: A non-profit that uses science-based programs to empower consumers, purchasers, and companies to create a more sustainable world.

   - Website: https://www.greenseal.org/

3. The Local Food Movement: An online platform dedicated to connecting consumers with local farmers.

   - Website: https://www.localfoodmovement.org/

4. Global Reporting Initiative: Provides sustainability reporting standards.

   - Website: https://www.globalreporting.org/

## Recommended Readings

1. "The Responsibility Revolution" by Jeffrey Hollender and Bill Breen

   - A deep dive into how companies can lead with their values and build better businesses.

2. "Green to Gold" by Daniel C. Esty and Andrew S. Winston

   - How smart companies use environmental strategies to innovate, create value, and build competitive advantage.

3. "Sustainable Logistics and Supply Chain Management" by David B. Grant, Alexander Trautrims, and Chee Yew Wong

   - A comprehensive insight into the key issues and challenges of green logistics and supply chain management.

4. "Slow Food: The Case for Taste" by Carlo Petrini

   - Discusses the principles behind the Slow Food Movement, which supports local, sustainable agriculture.

5. "The Omnivore's Dilemma" by Michael Pollan

   - An exploration into the ethics and realities of our modern food system.

6. "The Building Decarbonization Practice Guide" – The William J. Worthen Foundation

- Offers a comprehensive understanding of the implications of building decarbonization. Serves as a practical resource for professionals in construction & hospitality sectors aiming to adopt sustainable building practices.

## Studies

1. "The Economic Impacts of Local Food Systems"

   - A study exploring the economic viability of local food systems compared to traditional supply chains.

2. "The Value of Green Labeling in the Hospitality Industry"

   - A study that assesses the importance of eco-labeling for customer choices in the hospitality sector.

3. "Sustainability in Supply Chain Management: A Literature Review"

   - An academic review of sustainability initiatives in supply chain management across industries.

4. "The Role of CSR in the Hospitality Industry"

   - A study that delves into how Corporate Social Responsibility (CSR) practices impact consumer choices and business operations in the hospitality industry.

5. "Lifecycle Analysis of Food Products: A Comparative Study"

   - Compares the environmental impacts of various foods based on lifecycle analysis criteria.

# Chapter 8

## Glossary of Key Terms

1. **Circular Economy**: An economic model designed to minimize waste and make the most of available resources.

2. **Eco-Efficiency**: A term that describes business operations that create economic value while reducing ecological impact.

3. **Waste Hierarchy**: A framework that prioritizes waste management options based on their environmental impact, from most favorable to least favorable.

4. **Resource Recovery**: The practice of extracting useful materials from waste.

5. **Zero-Waste**: A philosophy and set of practices aimed at eliminating waste by reusing and recycling materials.

6. **Upcycling**: The practice of taking something that is disposable and transforming it into something of greater use and value.

7. **Greenhouse Gas Emissions**: The release of greenhouse gases into the atmosphere, which contribute to global warming and climate change.

8. **Carbon Footprint**: A measure of the total amount of carbon dioxide emissions that are directly and indirectly caused by an activity or operation.

## Online Resources

1. Zero Waste International Alliance: Provides information, guidelines, and certification standards for zero-waste businesses.

   - Website: http://zwia.org/

2. Circular Economy Toolkit: A set of tools and case studies to help businesses transition to a circular economy model.

   - Website: https://www.circulareconomytoolkit.org/

3. The Ellen MacArthur Foundation: A leader in accelerating the transition to a circular economy.

   - Website: https://www.ellenmacarthurfoundation.org/

4. Carbon Trust: Offers various tools to measure and reduce carbon footprints.

   - Website: https://www.carbontrust.com/

## Recommended Readings

1. "Cradle to Cradle: Remaking the Way We Make Things" by William McDonough & Michael Braungart

   - Discusses the principles of circular economy and sustainable design.

2. "The Circular Economy Handbook" by Peter Lacy, Jessica Long, and Wesley Spindler

   - A comprehensive guide to the principles and practical application of the circular economy.

3. "The Zero Waste Solution" by Paul Connett

   - Explains the principles and benefits of adopting a zero-waste strategy.

4. "The Upcycle" by William McDonough & Michael Braungart

   - A follow-up to "Cradle to Cradle," focusing on upcycling as a business strategy.

5. "Don't Even Think About It: Why Our Brains Are Wired to Ignore Climate Change" by George Marshall

   - Explores psychological reasons why society generally ignores or underestimates the issue of climate change.

6. "The Building Decarbonization Practice Guide" – The William J. Worthen Foundation

- Offers a comprehensive understanding of the implications of building decarbonization. Serves as a practical resource for professionals in construction & hospitality sectors aiming to adopt sustainable building practices.

## Studies

1. "Waste Management & Research in a Circular Economy"

   - A scientific paper that provides insights into waste management within a circular economy framework.

2. "Carbon Footprinting in the Hotel Industry"

   - A study that examines methods for reducing carbon emissions in hospitality establishments.

3. "Economic and Environmental Benefits of the Circular Economy"

   - Explores the long-term economic and environmental benefits of adopting circular economic models in various sectors.

4. "Zero-Waste Strategies and Their Impact on Business Efficiency"

   - Examines how zero-waste practices can improve operational efficiency and reduce costs.

5. "Impacts of Upcycling on Waste Management and Economy"

   - Analyzes the effectiveness of upcycling in reducing waste and promoting sustainable development.

# Chapter 9

## Glossary of Key Terms

1. **Sustainable Sourcing**: The procurement of goods and services that are produced and supplied in an environmentally and socially responsible manner.

2. **Local Sourcing**: Procurement of goods and services from local suppliers to minimize transportation costs and carbon footprint.

3. **Fair Trade**: A trading partnership that seeks greater equity in international trade by providing better trading conditions and promoting sustainability.

4. **Organic Produce**: Food items that are grown without the use of synthetic fertilizers, pesticides, or genetically modified organisms.

5. **Supply Chain Transparency**: The full disclosure of information about the sourcing and production of goods, often to prove ethical or sustainable practices.

6. **Food Miles**: The distance food is transported from the time of its production to its arrival at the consumer.

7. **Greenwashing**: Disinformation disseminated by an organization to present an environmentally responsible public image.

8. **Renewable Energy Credits (RECs)**: Certificates that prove electricity was generated using renewable energy sources.

## Online Resources

1. Sustainable Procurement Resource Centre: Offers information and tools for businesses to switch to sustainable sourcing.

   - Website: https://www.sustainable-procurement.org/

2. Fair Trade Certified: Provides certification for Fair Trade products and a search tool to find them.

   - Website: https://www.fairtradecertified.org/

3. The Organic Center: A resource for scientific research and education on organic food and farming.

   - Website: https://www.organic-center.org/

4. ENERGY STAR: Provides tools and guidelines for sourcing energy-efficient appliances and systems.

   - Website: https://www.energystar.gov/

## Recommended Readings

1. "The Responsible Business: Reimagining Sustainability and Success" by Carol Sanford

   - Explores responsible sourcing and business ethics.

2. "The Green to Gold Business Playbook" by Daniel C. Esty and P.J. Simmons

   - Offers strategies for achieving environmental sustainability in various business contexts.

3. "Confessions of an Eco-Sinner" by Fred Pearce

   - Chronicles the author's journey to track down the sources of the items in his life, exposing a network of exploitation.

4. "Buying for Impact: How to Buy from Women and Change Our World" by Christine Schnitzer and Elizabeth L. Vazquez

   - Focuses on the role of gender in sustainable sourcing.

5. "Green Giants: How Smart Companies Turn Sustainability into Billion-Dollar Businesses" by E. Freya Williams

   - Highlights companies that have successfully integrated sustainability into their business models.

6. "The Building Decarbonization Practice Guide" – The William J. Worthen Foundation

- Offers a comprehensive understanding of the implications of building decarbonization. Serves as a practical resource for professionals in construction & hospitality sectors aiming to adopt sustainable building practices.

## Studies

1. "The Economic Feasibility of Sustainable Sourcing"

   - Investigates the cost-effectiveness of shifting to sustainable sourcing strategies.

2. "Environmental and Social Impacts of Local Sourcing"

   - Examines how local sourcing practices influence environmental sustainability and community development.

3. "The Truth Behind Food Miles: Local vs. Global Sourcing"

   - Compares the carbon footprint associated with local and global food sourcing.

4. "Effectiveness of Fair Trade Certifications in the Hospitality Sector"

   - Analyzes how Fair Trade certifications affect consumer perceptions and business practices.

5. "Greenwashing in the Supply Chain: Risks and Solutions"

   - Discusses the risks associated with greenwashing and proposes strategies to promote genuine sustainable practices.

# Chapter 10

## Glossary of Key Terms

1. **Carbon Footprint**: The amount of carbon dioxide and other carbon compounds emitted due to the consumption of fossil fuels.

2. **Energy Efficiency**: Using less energy to provide the same level of energy service.

3. **Sustainable Sourcing**: A procurement process that prioritizes the use of goods and services that have the least impact on the environment.

4. **Renewable Energy**: Energy generated from natural processes that are continuously replenished.

5. **Waste-to-Energy**: The process of generating energy in the form of electricity or heat from the primary treatment of waste.

6. **Eco-certification**: A certification scheme that verifies the eco-friendliness of products or services.

7. Circular Economy: An economic system aimed at eliminating waste through the continual use of resources.

## Online Resources

1. ENERGY STAR: Official site for ENERGY STAR ratings and certifications.

   - Website: https://www.energystar.gov/

2. Global Reporting Initiative (GRI): Provides standards for sustainability reporting.

   - Website: https://www.globalreporting.org/

3. Sustainable Restaurant Association: A not-for-profit organization helping restaurants become more sustainable.

   - Website: https://thesra.org/

## Recommended Readings

1. "Sustainable Hospitality and Tourism as Motors for Development: Case Studies from Developing Regions of the World" by Willy Legrand and Philip Sloan.

2. "Green to Gold: How Smart Companies Use Environmental Strategy to Innovate, Create Value, and Build a Competitive Advantage" by Daniel C. Esty and Andrew S. Winston.

3. "The Circular Economy Handbook: Realizing the Circular Advantage" by Peter Lacy, Jessica Long, and Wesley Spindler.

4. "The Building Decarbonization Practice Guide" – The William J. Worthen Foundation

- Offers a comprehensive understanding of the implications of building decarbonization. Serves as a practical resource for professionals in construction & hospitality sectors aiming to adopt sustainable building practices.

## Studies

1. "The Impact of Sustainability on the Food and Beverage Industry" - A 2019 study that explores how sustainability efforts directly affect consumer choices in the food and beverage sector.

2. "Evaluating the ROI of Sustainability in the Hospitality Industry" - A 2021 study that looks at the returns on investments in sustainable initiatives by hotels and restaurants.

3. "Sustainability in Supply Chain Management: A study on the Hospitality Industry" - Examines the role of sustainability in sourcing and supply chain management in the hospitality sector.

# Chapter 11

## Glossary of Key Terms

1. **Integrated Sustainability**: A holistic approach to sustainable development that incorporates environmental, social, and economic considerations.

2. **Carbon Footprint**: The total amount of greenhouse gases emitted directly or indirectly by human activities, usually expressed in equivalent tons of carbon dioxide ($CO_2e$).

3. **Circular Economy**: An economic system aimed at minimizing waste and making the most of available resources.

4. **Corporate Social Responsibility (CSR)**: A business model that helps a company be socially accountable—to itself, its stakeholders, and the public.

5. **Net-Zero Emissions**: A balance between the amount of greenhouse gas emissions produced and the amount removed from the atmosphere.

## Online Resources

1. CDPA not-for-profit that runs the global disclosure system for companies to measure their environmental impact.

   - Website: https://www.cdp.net/en

2. **Science Based Targets**: Provides companies with a pathway for reducing greenhouse gas emissions.

   - Website: https://sciencebasedtargets.org/

3. **The Circular Economy Toolkit**: A resource for businesses wanting to engage in more circular practices.

   - Website: https://www.circulareconomytoolkit.org/

## Recommended Readings

1. "The Circular Economy Handbook: Realizing the Circular Advantage" by Peter Lacy, Jessica Long, and Wesley Spindler.

2. "Sustainability for Hospitality: Best Practices and Trends" by Cathy Hsu and Willy Legrand.

3. "The New Climate Economy" by Helen Clarkson, which discusses the economic benefits of transitioning to a sustainable business model.

4. "The Building Decarbonization Practice Guide" — The William J. Worthen Foundation

- Offers a comprehensive understanding of the implications of building decarbonization. Serves as a practical resource for professionals in construction & hospitality sectors aiming to adopt sustainable building practices.

**Studies**

1. "Measuring the ROI of Sustainability Initiatives"- A 2021 study examining the long-term economic benefits of sustainability initiatives in the business sector.

2. "From Linear to Circular: Transitioning to a Sustainable Economy" - A 2020 study looking at case studies of businesses that have successfully transitioned to a circular economy model.

3. "Corporate Social Responsibility and Financial Performance" - This study delves into the impact of CSR activities on a company's bottom line, particularly within the context of the hospitality sector.

# Chapter 12

**Glossary of Key Terms**

1. **Eco-Conscious Traveler**: A traveler who makes choices with sustainability and the environment in mind.

2. **Smart Sustainability**: The use of data analytics and artificial intelligence to enhance sustainable practices.

3. **Green Initiatives**: Programs and strategies aimed at promoting sustainable and environmentally friendly practices.

4. **Regulatory Compliance**: Adhering to laws, regulations, guidelines, or specifications relevant to the business.

5. **Operational Efficiency**: The capability of an enterprise to deliver products or services to its customers in the most cost-effective manner possible while maintaining the quality of the product or service.

## Online Resources

1. Green Key: An eco-label awarded to thousands of establishments in hospitality worldwide.

   - Website: https://www.greenkey.global/

2. ENERGY STAR for Hotels: Resources to improve energy efficiency and save money.

   - Website: https://www.energystar.gov/buildings/facility-owners-and-managers/small-biz/hospitality

3. Sustainable Hospitality Alliance: Organization that helps hotels become more sustainable.

   - Website: https://sustainablehospitalityalliance.org/

4. LEED Certification for Hospitality: Information on how LEED works specifically for the hospitality industry.

- Website: https://www.usgbc.org/

## Recommended Readings

1. "Sustainable Hospitality: Principles and Practices" by Philip Sloan, Willy Legrand, and Joseph S. Chen.

2. "The Future of Sustainable Travel: Ethical, Economic and Social Implications" by Xavier Font and Scott McCabe.

3. "Hospitality 2050: The Future of Hospitality and Travel" by Ian Yeoman and Una McMahon-Beattie.

4. "The Building Decarbonization Practice Guide" – The William J. Worthen Foundation

- Offers a comprehensive understanding of the implications of building decarbonization. Serves as a practical resource for professionals in construction & hospitality sectors aiming to adopt sustainable building practices.

## Studies

1. "The Role of Artificial Intelligence in Achieving the Sustainable Development Goals" - A 2021 study exploring how AI can contribute to sustainability in various industries, including hospitality.

2. "The Business Case for Eco-Certification in Hospitality" - A 2020 study examining the return on investment for hotels that become eco-certified.

3. "Consumer Preferences and the Impact on Sustainability Practices in Hospitality" - A 2022 study that delves into how

consumer demand is driving the adoption of sustainability practices in the hospitality industry.

This appendix serves to expand on the content of this textbook, offering additional resources and readings for those interested in delving deeper into the topics of sustainable procurement, local sourcing, and green supply chain management in the hospitality industry.

Made in the USA
Columbia, SC
22 March 2024